BOOK OF

SUCCESSFUL
HOME PLANS

BOOK OF
SUCCESSFUL
HOME PLANS

Designs by
Richard Pollman

STRUCTURES PUBLISHING COMPANY 1976
Farmington, Michigan

Manufactured in the United States of America

Edited by Shirley M. Horowitz

Current Printing (last digit)
10 9 8 7 6 5 4 3 2 1

International Standard Book Number: 0-912336-34-X (cloth)
0-912336-35-8 (paper)

Library of Congress Catalog Card Number: 76-23485

Structures Publishing Co.
Box 423, Farmington, Mich. 48024

CONTENTS

FOREWORD

Buyers of our Successful Series of books on Kitchens, Bathrooms, Space Saving, How to Build Your Own Home and others have expressed a desire for a book of home plans from which they can select a home to suit their particular needs. At the same time, those whose needs cannot be served by stock plans can use those included as a jumping off point for their more customized planning.

The book is divided into two sections. In the first part, we provide some of the criteria used by HUD (U. S. Dept. of Housing and Urban Development) in checking the feasibility of floor plans and adequacy of other design considerations. In the second part, we bring you 226 plans of homes designed by Richard B. Pollman. These plans are currently the most popular among the hundreds of stock plans available from Home Planners, Inc.

SECTION I: Design Criteria

Diagrams shown are from the *Manual of Acceptable Practices* prepared by the U. S. Department of Housing and Urban Development, publication #4730.1.

On the first six pages of this section we have included some of the important design and furniture placement features you should consider in selecting a plan or designing a custom plan from the beginning. The furniture sizes and room layouts are all to ¼" scale (¼" = 1'0" on the plan), as are most blueprints. Not included are arrangements for queen-size (60" X 80") or king-size beds (78" X 80"). Any floor plan that you consider or develop for your own use should be checked against these minimum sizes and clearances. Keep in mind that these are minimums, and your life style may require greater clearances. Of course, if your conversation grouping in your living room becomes much larger than the 10-foot diameter circle shown, you may have difficulty communicating with your guests.

SECTION II: 226 Home Plans, designs by Richard B. Pollman

The founder of Home Planners, Inc. in 1946, Pollman has a national reputation as one of the country's outstanding home designers. Mr. Pollman's work has been known to millions of readers of leading shelter magazines and trade publications. His houses have been acclaimed for the distinctiveness of their exterior appeal. Exquisite proportion and simplicity of design have become the hallmark of Pollman design.

The designs in this book include 72 one-story homes, 26 one- and one-half story homes, 60 two-story homes, 39 multi-level homes, including split levels, bi-levels and hillsides and 29 vacation homes including A-frames and Chalets.

This section concludes with several pages of information as to how you can order the modestly priced plans and specifications for any home you may select.

Although Structures selected Home Planners, Inc. to work with in preparing this book, there are other plan services whom you may wish to contact in order to broaden your choice of stock plans. We recommend the following:

Garlinghouse Co., Inc.
2320 Kansas Ave.
Topeka, Kansas 66611

Home Building Plan Service, Inc.
2235 N. E. Sandy Blvd.
Portland, Oregon 97232

Master Plan Service
89 East Jericho Turnpike
Mineola, New York 11501

R. J. Lytle
Publisher

INDEX TO DESIGNS

DESIGN CRITERIA

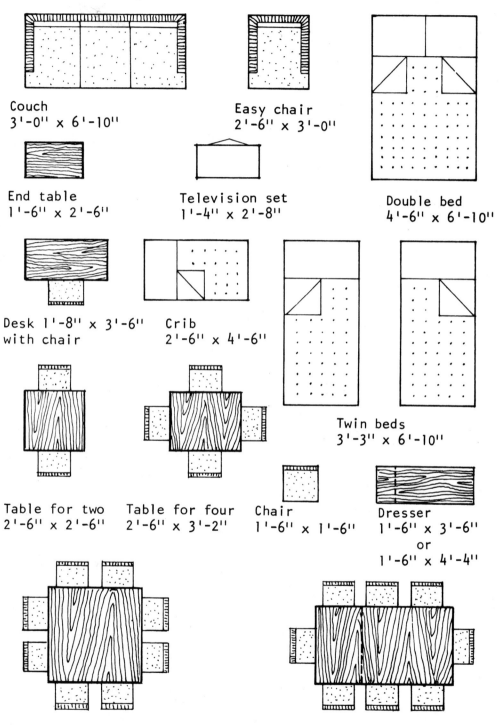

Couch
3'-0" x 6'-10"

Easy chair
2'-6" x 3'-0"

End table
1'-6" x 2'-6"

Television set
1'-4" x 2'-8"

Double bed
4'-6" x 6'-10"

Desk 1'-8" x 3'-6"
with chair

Crib
2'-6" x 4'-6"

Twin beds
3'-3" x 6'-10"

Table for two
2'-6" x 2'-6"

Table for four
2'-6" x 3'-2"

Chair
1'-6" x 1'-6"

Dresser
1'-6" x 3'-6"
or
1'-6" x 4'-4"

Dining table with chairs for six = 3'-4" x 4'-0"
for eight = 3'-4" x 6'-0" or 4'-0" x 4'-0"

9

LIVING AREA

Planning Considerations

Thru traffic should be separated from activity centers.

Openings should be located so as to give enough wall space for various furniture arrangements.

Convenient access should be provided to doors, windows, electric outlets, thermostats and supply grills.

Furniture Clearances

To assure adequate space for convenient use of furniture in the living area, not less than the following clearances should be observed.

> 60" between facing seating
> 24" where circulation occurs between furniture
> 30" for use of desk
> 36" for main traffic
> 60" between television set and seating

Seating arranged around a 10 ft diameter circle makes a comfortable grouping for conversation.

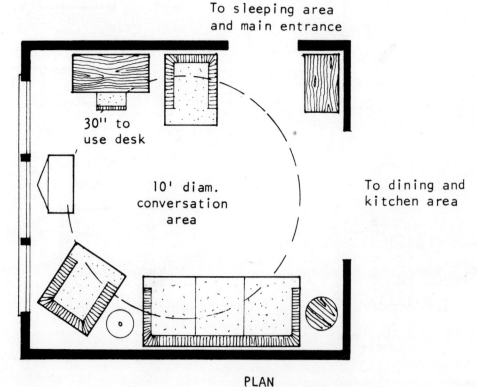

To sleeping area
and main entrance

30" to
use desk

10' diam.
conversation
area

To dining and
kitchen area

PLAN

DINING AREA

Furniture Clearances

To assure adequate space for convenient use of the dining area, not less than the following clearances from the edge of the dining table should be observed.

32" for chairs plus access thereto
38" for chairs plus access and passage
42" for serving from behind chair
24" for passage only
48" from table to base cabinet (in dining-kitchen)

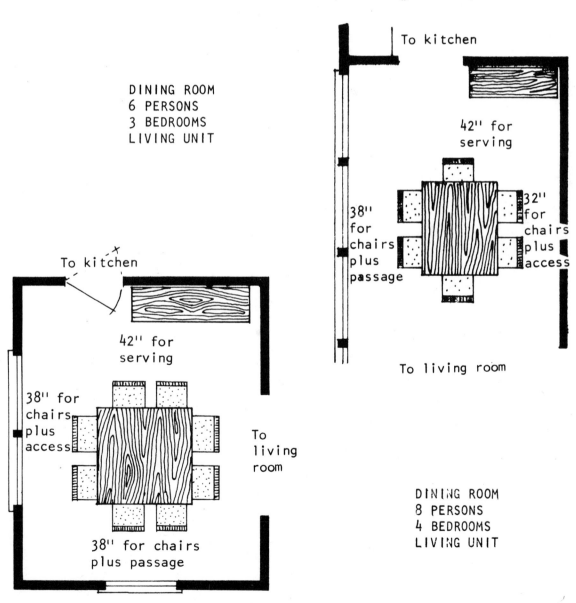

DINING ROOM
6 PERSONS
3 BEDROOMS
LIVING UNIT

To kitchen

42" for
serving

38"
for
chairs
plus
passage

32"
for
chairs
plus
access

To living room

To kitchen

42" for
serving

38" for
chairs
plus
access

To
living
room

38" for chairs
plus passage

DINING ROOM
8 PERSONS
4 BEDROOMS
LIVING UNIT

Furniture Clearances

To assure adequate space for convenient use of furniture in the bedroom,
not less than the following clearances should be observed.

> 42" at one side or foot of bed for dressing
> 6" between side of bed and side of dresser or chest
> 36" in front of dresser, closet and chest of drawers
> 24" for major circulation path (door to closet, etc.)
> 22" on one side of bed for circulation
> 12" on least used side of double bed. The least used side of
>   a single or twin bed can be placed against the wall except
>   in bedrooms for the elderly.

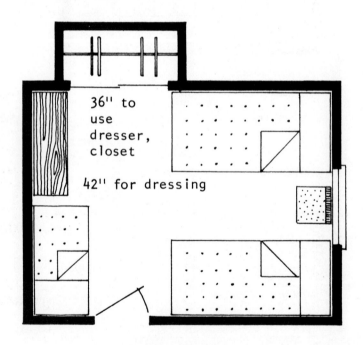

PRIMARY BEDROOM

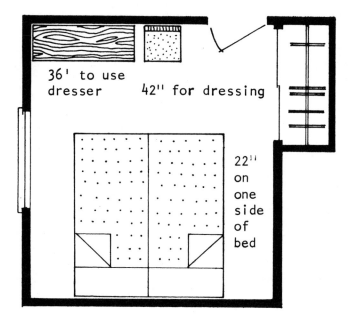

36' to use dresser

42" for dressing

22" on one side of bed

PRIMARY BEDROOM WITHOUT CRIB

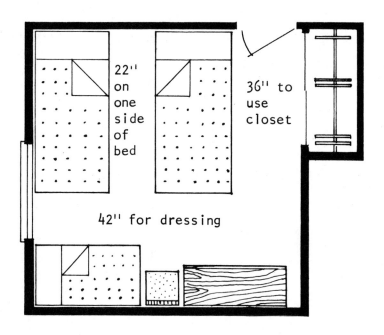

22" on one side of bed

36" to use closet

42" for dressing

PRIMARY BEDROOM

BEDROOMS

The location of doors and windows should permit alternate furniture arrangements.

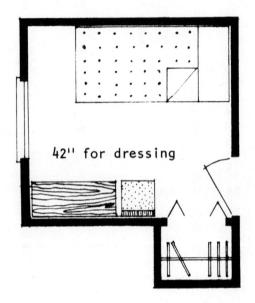

42" for dressing

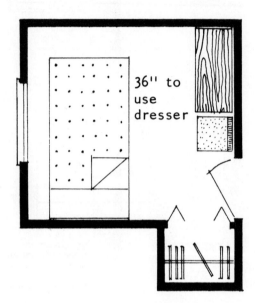

36" to use dresser

SINGLE OCCUPANCY BEDROOM

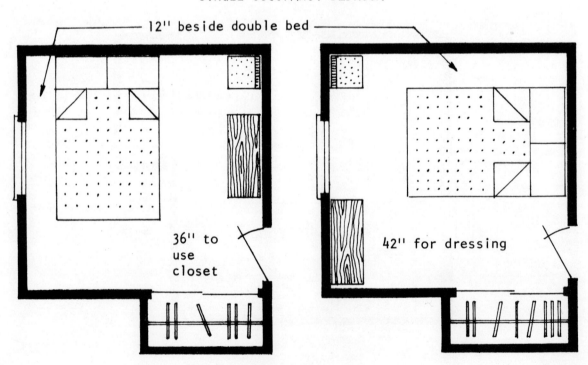

12" beside double bed

36" to use closet

42" for dressing

DOUBLE OCCUPANCY BEDROOM

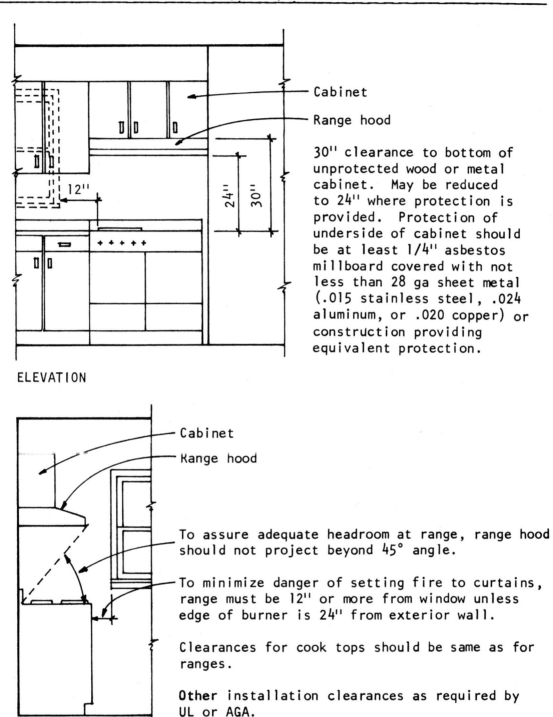

Cabinet

Range hood

30" clearance to bottom of unprotected wood or metal cabinet. May be reduced to 24" where protection is provided. Protection of underside of cabinet should be at least 1/4" asbestos millboard covered with not less than 28 ga sheet metal (.015 stainless steel, .024 aluminum, or .020 copper) or construction providing equivalent protection.

ELEVATION

Cabinet

Range hood

To assure adequate headroom at range, range hood should not project beyond 45° angle.

To minimize danger of setting fire to curtains, range must be 12" or more from window unless edge of burner is 24" from exterior wall.

Clearances for cook tops should be same as for ranges.

Other installation clearances as required by UL or AGA.

SECTION

RANGE CLEARANCES

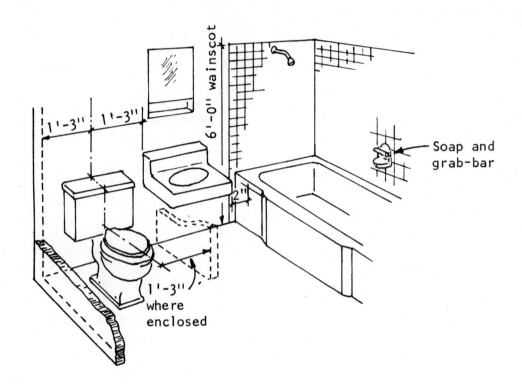

1'-3" 1'-3"

6'-0" wainscot

Soap and grab-bar

2"

1'-3" where enclosed

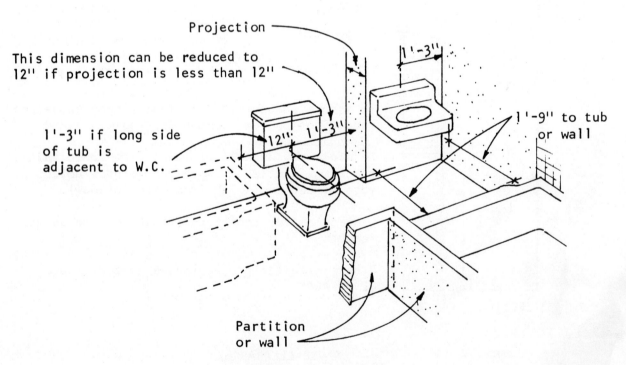

Projection

This dimension can be reduced to 12" if projection is less than 12"

1'-3" if long side of tub is adjacent to W.C.

12" 1'-3"

1'-3"

1'-9" to tub or wall

Partition or wall

CLEARANCES FOR BATHROOMS

CLOSETS IN LIVING UNITS

Clothes rods should be mounted at least 5'-0" clear of floor or obstructions but not more than 6'-8" above floor.

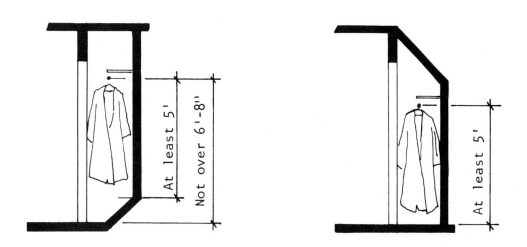

COMMON STORAGE AREAS FOR MULTIFAMILY HOUSING

Common storage areas should be appropriately divided into compartments or closets for each living unit. Storage areas less than 1 ft in depth or less than 4 ft in height and portions of closets more than 8 ft in height should not be included in required volume. Compartments should not exceed 4 ft in depth unless a 2 ft wide access space is provided.

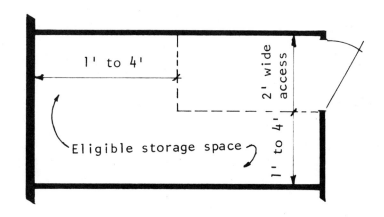

GENERAL STORAGE COMPARTMENT
IN A COMMON STORAGE ROOM

NATURAL LIGHTING

Measure of Window Light Area

In determining required natural light area, measure the actual glass area disregarding muntins.

Natural Light at Porches

When an opening providing required natural light opens onto a covered porch whose depth exceeds 4 feet, the opening should be increased in area 10 percent for each foot of depth over 4 feet, except if the side of the projected porch covering is within 4 ft from any edge of the opening providing natural light, no increase is necessary.

Recommended Maximum Depth of Rooms

The depth "D" of a room from a window wall should not be more than 2 1/2 times the height "H" of the window head. The depth "D" may be increased when a side window is provided or when more than the minimum amount of natural light is provided.

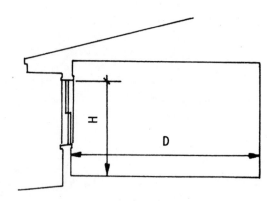

Recommended Minimum Illumination for Dwellings

The following table shows levels of illumination for safety in and around the dwelling.

Location	Footcandles
General Lighting	
For safety in passage area (Halls & stairs)	hall 5, stairs 10
Areas primarily for relaxation	10
Areas involving visual task	30
Entrances and exterior steps	5
Exterior walkway surface	1
Specific visual tasks	
Kitchen activities	
Sink	70
Range and work surfaces	50
Laundry activities	
Ironing	50
Washer and dryer	30
Bathroom at the mirror	50

ARTIFICIAL LIGHTING

Stair Lighting

Stairs rank high as causes of accidents in dwellings. One way to
reduce the number of accidents is to have adequate light that does
not cast shadows upon the treads.

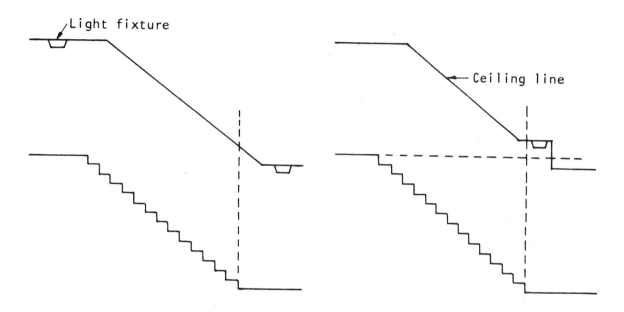

To accomplish this provide a light fixture at top and bottom of stairs
and use a light reflective color on the ceiling. The bottom fixture
should be beyond the lowest riser.

One fixture is adequate when located higher than the top riser and
beyond the bottom riser. This location produces a shadow of a person
ascending the stairs. However, this is the less hazardous direction of
travel. A soft diffused light should be used to prevent a glare that
might blind a person descending the stairs.

INTERIOR STAIRS

Design Suggestions

Use of slip resistant treads is recommended.

Use of open risers is discouraged (their use is not permitted in housing for the elderly and handicapped and in care-type housing).

Use of overly large, toe-catching nosings is discouraged in housing for the elderly and handicapped.

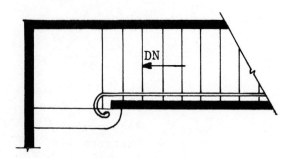

**FLIGHT OF TWO RISERS
PUBLIC OR PRIVATE STAIRS**

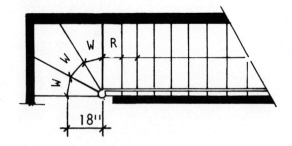

WINDERS, PRIVATE STAIRS

W cannot be less than
R for typical run

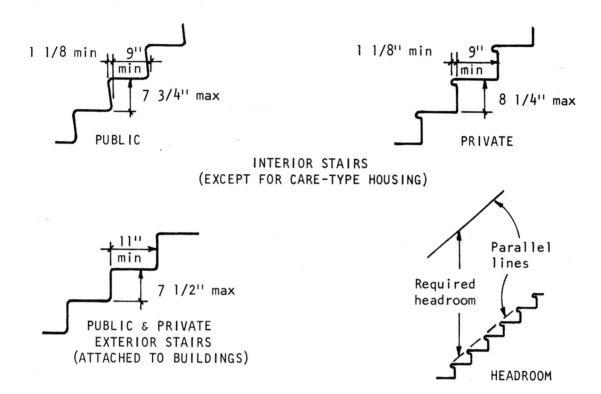

INTERIOR STAIRS
(EXCEPT FOR CARE-TYPE HOUSING)

PUBLIC

1 1/8 min   9" min   7 3/4" max

PRIVATE

1 1/8" min   9" min   8 1/4" max

PUBLIC & PRIVATE
EXTERIOR STAIRS
(ATTACHED TO BUILDINGS)

11" min   7 1/2" max

HEADROOM

Parallel lines

Required headroom

SECTIONS OF STAIRS
(SHOWING MANDATORY LIMITATIONS)

HANDRAIL AND RAILING DETAILS

Handrails should be placed on the right side of stairs, descending.
Horizontal dimension of handrail (grip) should not exceed 2 5/8".
Handrails should return to wall or floor, or terminate in a post,
scroll or loop (mandatory for housing for elderly or handicapped).
Mounting height for stairs handrails should be 30" to 34". Railing
height for stoops, porches, etc. should be at least 30" (42" mandatory
for exterior corridors, balconies, roof decks).

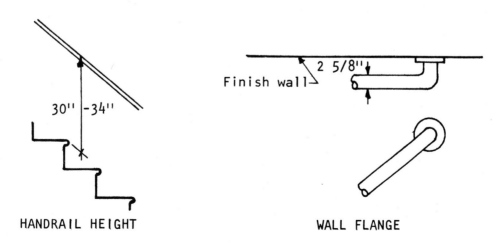

HANDRAIL HEIGHT

30"-34"

WALL FLANGE

Finish wall

2 5/8"

Attic vents entirely in eave or entirely
near the ridge are acceptable means of ventilation.
However a combination of eave and ridge ventilation is
desirable to provide a thermal head to induce
air flow.

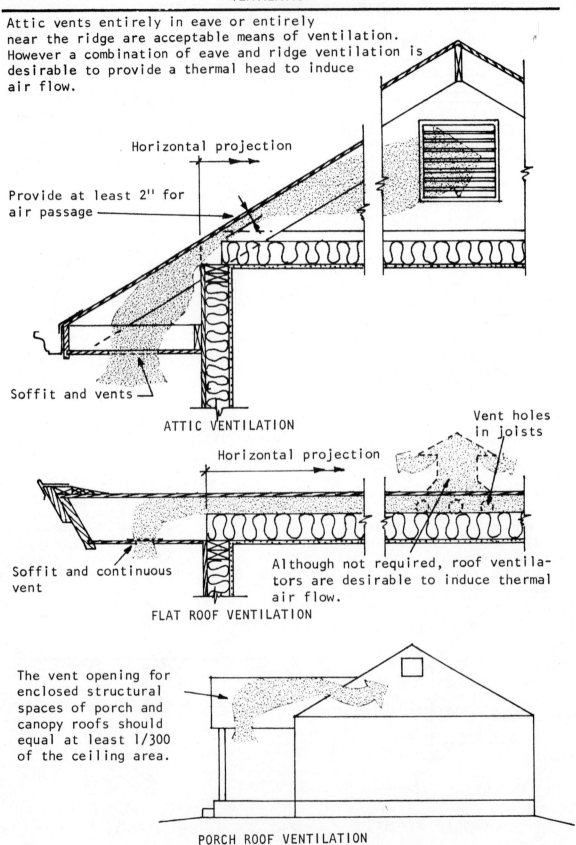

Horizontal projection

Provide at least 2" for
air passage

Soffit and vents

ATTIC VENTILATION

Horizontal projection

Vent holes
in joists

Soffit and continuous
vent

Although not required, roof ventilators are desirable to induce thermal
air flow.

FLAT ROOF VENTILATION

The vent opening for
enclosed structural
spaces of porch and
canopy roofs should
equal at least 1/300
of the ceiling area.

PORCH ROOF VENTILATION

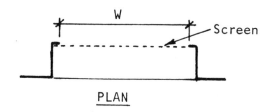

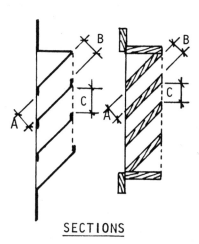

SECTIONS

PLAN

Formula

Net free area = number of openings times
W times the smallest of the following:
    dimension A or B or C x 0.8*

* average net area for 8 x 8 mesh
galvanized or aluminum screen

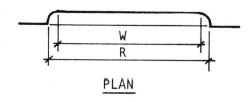

PLAN

Formula

Net free area = number of openings
times W times the smallest of the
following: dimension A or B
             or C x 0.8 or
             D + E x 0.8
W = R minus 0.4A

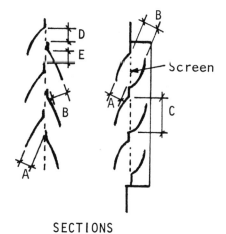

SECTIONS

NET FREE AREA OF VENTILATING OPENINGS

Porches

Doors and windows which open to a glass enclosed porch may be included in required ventilating area when the required area is provided in both the exterior wall and porch.

Bath

The least amount of natural ventilation opening area should be 3 sq ft unless mechanical ventilation is provided.

Any compartment containing a fixture and opening into the bathroom is considered a part of that bathroom and does not require separate ventilation.

Attic Spaces

Attic spaces which are accessible and suitable for future habitable rooms or walled-off storage space should have at least 50 percent of the required ventilating area located in the upper part of the space as near to the high point of the roof as practicable and above the probable level of any future ceiling. All openings should be protected against the entrance of snow and rain.

Basementless Spaces (Crawl Spaces)

Foundation wall ventilators are not required for basementless space when one side, exclusive of structural supports, is completely open to a basement; except that basementless spaces having an area greater than the basement should be separately ventilated.

Screening

All exterior openings used for ventilating such spaces as attics and crawl spaces should be screened with at least 8 mesh per inch screening.

Traditional & Contemporary
One-Story Homes

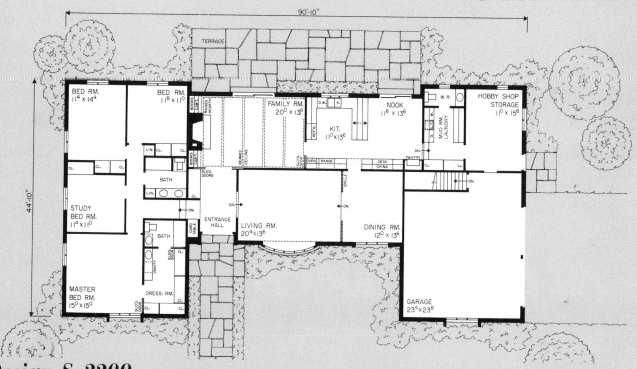

Design S 2209   2,659 Sq. Ft./45,240 Cu. Ft.

Such an impressive home would, indeed, be difficult to top. And little wonder when you consider the myriad of features this one-story Colonial has going for it. Consider the exquisite detailing, the fine proportions, and the symmetry of the projecting wings. The gracious and inviting double front doors are a prelude to the exceptional interior. For the growing, active family there are features galore. Consider the four bedroom, two-bath sleeping wing. There are plenty of closets and a big dressing room. Then for formal entertaining there are the front living and dining rooms. For informal living there is the rear family room. The homemaker will find her work center a joy in which to function. All will love the hobby shop. If you wish, this can be ideal for storage of bulk items.

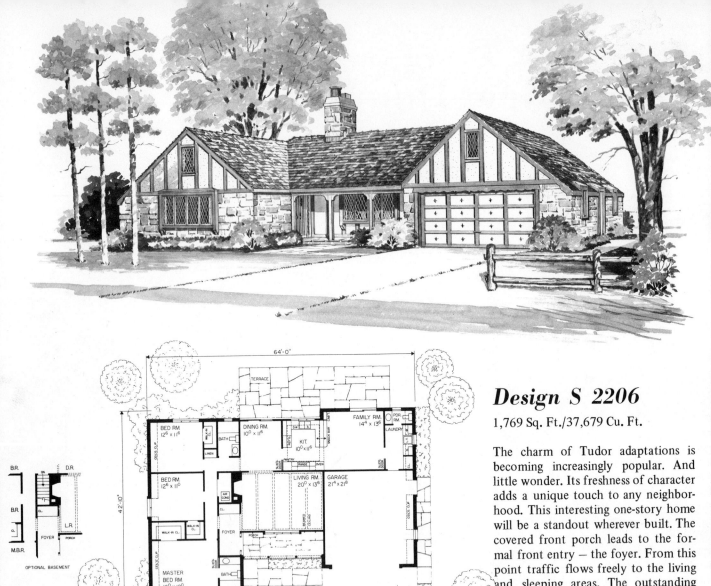

Design S 2206

1,769 Sq. Ft./37,679 Cu. Ft.

The charm of Tudor adaptations is becoming increasingly popular. And little wonder. Its freshness of character adds a unique touch to any neighborhood. This interesting one-story home will be a standout wherever built. The covered front porch leads to the formal front entry — the foyer. From this point traffic flows freely to the living and sleeping areas. The outstanding plan features three bedrooms, with two full baths, walk-in closets, a separate dining room, a beamed ceiling living room and efficient kitchen, and an informal family room.

Design S 1989

2,282 Sq. Ft./41,831 Cu. Ft.

High style with a plan as contemporary as today and tomorrow. There is, indeed, a feeling of coziness that emanates from the ground-hugging qualities of this picturesque home. Inside, there is livability galore. There's the four bedroom, two bath sleeping wing with a dressing room as a bonus. There's the sunken living room and the separate dining room to function as the family's formal living area. Then, over-looking the rear yard, there's the informal living area with its beamed ceiling family room and wonderful kitchen with adjacent breakfast room.

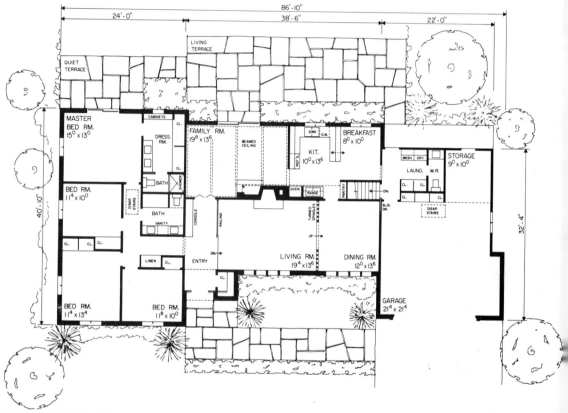

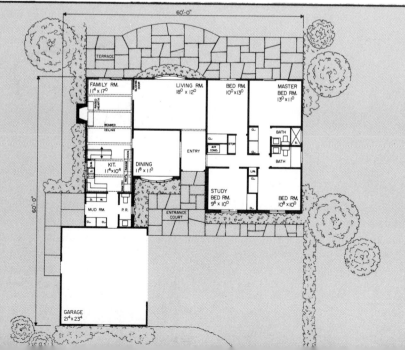

Design S 2170

1,646 Sq. Ft./22,034 Cu. Ft.

An L-shape home with an enchanting Olde English styling. The wavy-edged siding, the similated beams, the diamond lite windows, the unusual brick pattern, and the interesting lines all are elements which set the character of authenticity. The center entry routes traffic directly to the formal living and sleeping zones of the house. Between the kitchen-family room area and the attached two-car garage is the mud room. Here is the washer and dryer with extra powder room nearby.

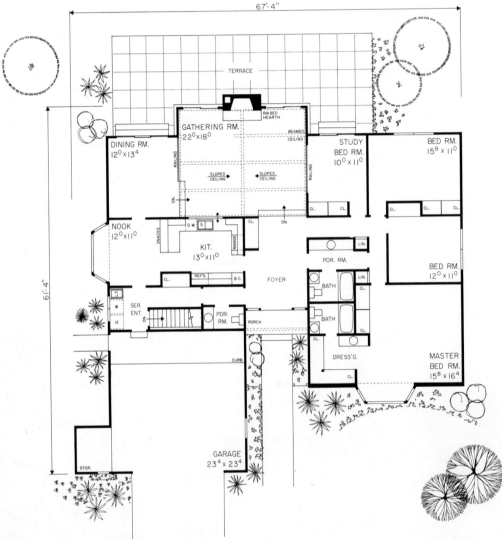

Design S 2527 2,392 Sq. Ft. / 42,579 Cu. Ft.

Vertical boards and battens, fieldstone, bay window, a dovecote, a gas lamp, and a recessed front entrance are among the appealing exterior features of this U-shaped design. Through the double front doors flanked by glass side lites one enters the spacious foyer. Straight ahead is the cozy sunken gathering room with its sloping, beamed ceiling, raised hearth fireplace, and two sets of sliding glass doors to the rear terrace. To the right of the foyer is the sleeping wing with its three bedrooms, study (make it the fourth bedroom if you wish), and two baths. To the left is the strategically located powder room and large kitchen with its delightful nook space and bay window.

What a pleasing, traditional exterior. And what a fine, Convenient Living interior! The configuration of this home leads to interesting roof planes and even functional outdoor terrace areas. The front court and the covered porch with its stolid pillars strike an enchanting note. The gathering room will be just that. It will be the family's multi-purpose living area. Sunken to a level of two steps its already spacious feeling is enhanced by its open planning with the dining room and study. This latter room may be closed off for more privacy if desired. Just adjacent to the foyer is the open stairwell to the basement level. Here will be the possibility of developing recreation space.

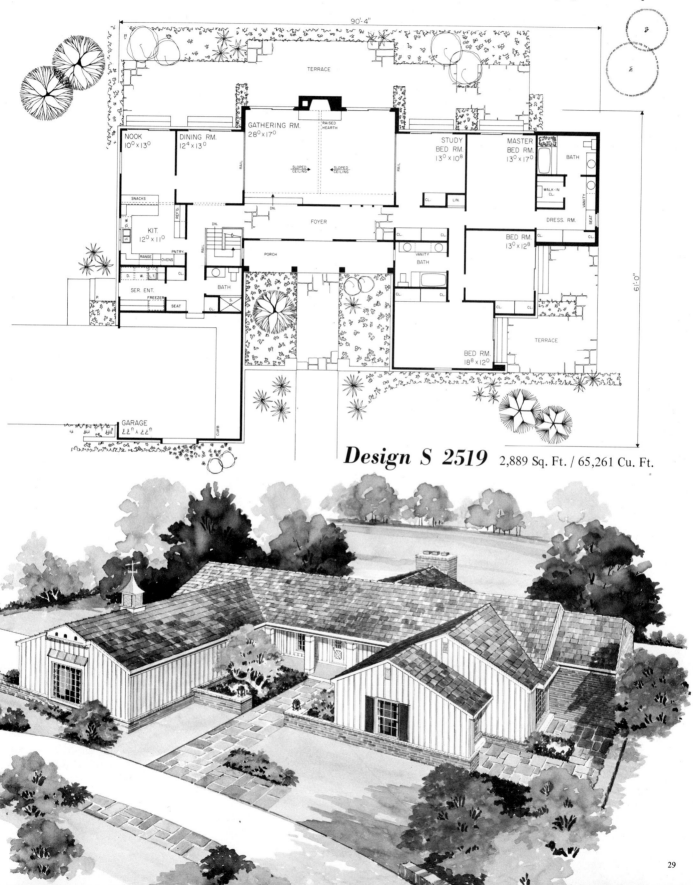

Design S 2519 2,889 Sq. Ft. / 65,261 Cu. Ft.

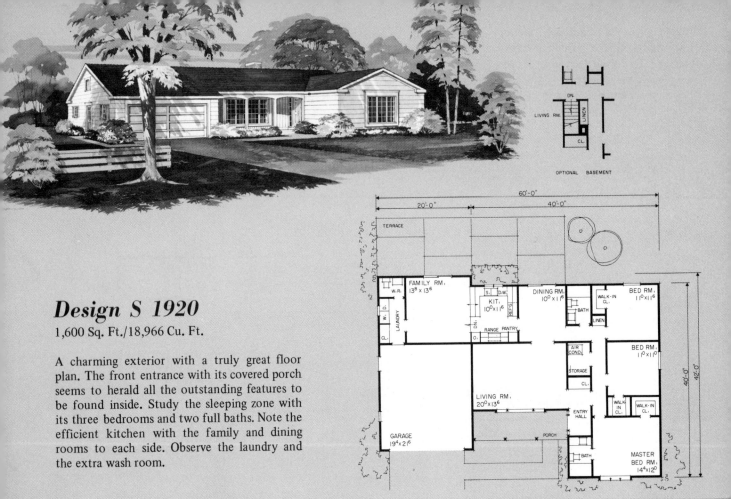

Design S 1920

1,600 Sq. Ft./18,966 Cu. Ft.

A charming exterior with a truly great floor plan. The front entrance with its covered porch seems to herald all the outstanding features to be found inside. Study the sleeping zone with its three bedrooms and two full baths. Note the efficient kitchen with the family and dining rooms to each side. Observe the laundry and the extra wash room.

OPTIONAL BASEMENT

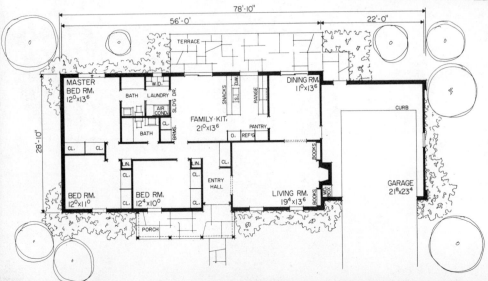

Design S 1890

1,628 Sq. Ft./20,350 Cu. Ft.

The pediment gable and columns help set the charm of this modestly sized home. Here is graciousness normally associated with homes twice its size. The pleasant symmetry of the windows and the double front doors complete the picture. Inside, each square foot is wisely planned to assure years of convenient living. There are three bedrooms, each with twin wardrobe closets.

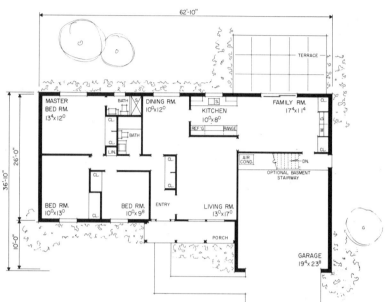

Design S 1305

1,382 Sq. Ft./16,584 Cu. Ft.

Here is a plan that has, in less than 1,400 square feet, three bedrooms, two full baths, a separate dining room, a formal living room, a fine kitchen overlooking the rear yard, and an informal family room. In addition, there is the attached two-car garage. Note the location of the stairs when this plan is built with a basement. Study pleasing window treatment.

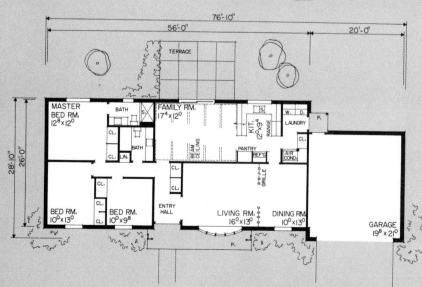

Design S 1388

1,488 Sq. Ft./18,600 Cu. Ft.

This beautiful exterior provides exceptional livability for the medium budget. In less than 1,500 square feet it would be difficult to recreate any greater degree of livability. The center entry hall routes traffic directly to the three main areas of the house — the formal living and dining area, the sleeping area, and the informal family living area. The U-shaped kitchen, with its pass-thru to the family room, has an abundance of storage facilities.

Design S 1761

2,548 Sq. Ft./43,870 Cu. Ft.

Low, strong roof lines and solid, enduring qualities of brick give this house a permanent, here-to-stay appearance. Bedroom wing is isolated, and the baths and closets deaden noise from the rest of the house. Center fireplaces in family and living rooms make furniture arrangement easy. There are a number of extras — a workshop, an unusually large garage, and an indoor barbecue. Garage has easy access to both basement and kitchen area. There are two eating areas — a formal dining room and a nook next to the delightful kitchen.

Design S 2181

2,612 Sq. Ft./45,230 Cu. Ft.

It is hard to imagine a home with any more eye-appeal than this one. It is the complete picture of charm. The interior is no less outstanding. Sliding glass doors permit the large master bedroom, the quiet living room, and the all-purpose family room to function directly with the outdoors. The two fireplaces, the built-in china cabinets, the book shelves, the complete laundry, the kitchen pass-thru to breakfast room are extra features. Count the closets. There are all kinds of storage facilities.

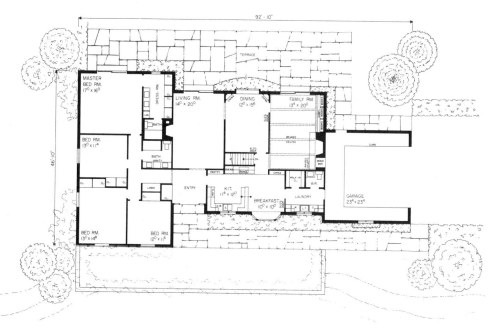

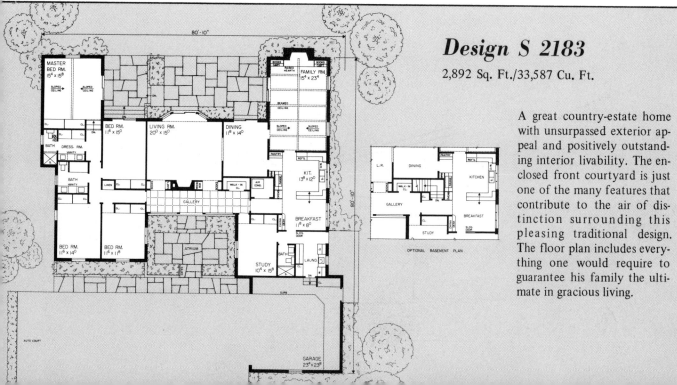

Design S 2183

2,892 Sq. Ft./33,587 Cu. Ft.

A great country-estate home with unsurpassed exterior appeal and positively outstanding interior livability. The enclosed front courtyard is just one of the many features that contribute to the air of distinction surrounding this pleasing traditional design. The floor plan includes everything one would require to guarantee his family the ultimate in gracious living.

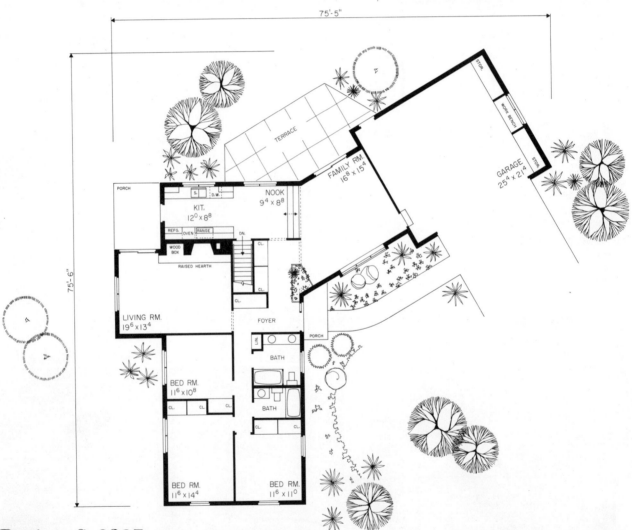

Design S 2327   1,820 Sq. Ft. / 26,897 Cu. Ft.

You will have fun deciding which orientation on your site you most prefer for this brick veneer home. Its angular shape provides just the right touch to assure an air of distinction. The center foyer routes traffic effectively. There is no unnecessary cross-room traffic in this design. The living room, with access to the rear privacy porch, features an appealing raised hearth fireplace wall. Acting as a divider between the nook and family room is a counter with cabinets above and below. A pass-thru provides direct access to each room. Should you wish, you may opt for having the family room function as the dining room. The built-in planter is an attractive highlight.

Design S 2265 1,861 Sq. Ft. / 36,888 Cu. Ft.

Inside and outside this home will provide a lifetime of satisfaction for its occupants. Whether called upon to serve the family's needs as a two or three bedroom home, it will do so with great merit. As a two bedroom home, there is then a quiet study with built-in desk, cabinets, and book shelves. The front-to-rear living room is 23 feet long and functions through sliding glass doors right out onto the terrace. Around the corner from the fireplace is the formal dining room. It, too, but a step from the terrace. The in-line kitchen will be efficient and function with breakfast nook. Note built-in china cabinets, pantry, wood box, vanity, linen storage, and basement.

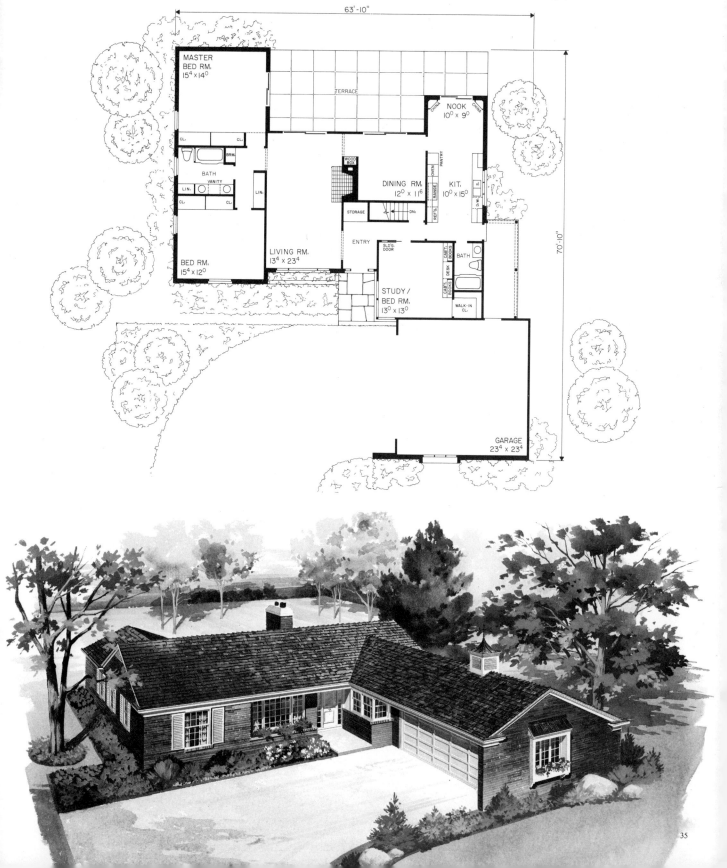

Design S 1380

1,399 Sq. Ft./17,937 Cu. Ft.

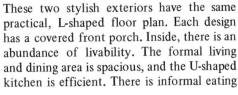

These two stylish exteriors have the same practical, L-shaped floor plan. Each design has a covered front porch. Inside, there is an abundance of livability. The formal living and dining area is spacious, and the U-shaped kitchen is efficient. There is informal eating

space, a separate laundry and a fine family room. Note the sliding glass doors to the terrace. The blueprints include details for building either with or without a basement. Observe the pantry of the non-basement plan. The storage of staples will be handy.

Design S 1381

1,399 Sq. Ft./17,937 Cu. Ft.

Design S 1346

1,644 Sq. Ft./19,070 Cu. Ft.

Whether you enter through the service door of the attached garage, or through the centered front entry your appreciation of what this plan has to offer will grow. The mud room area is certainly an outstanding feature. The housewife will welcome the location of the washer and dryer, the handy coat closet, and the extra wash room — particulary during inclement weather. Traffic flows from this area to the informal family room with its fireplace and access to the rear terrace. The efficient, strategically located kitchen looks out upon the yard.

Design S 1357

1,258 Sq. Ft./13,606 Cu. Ft.

Here is a relatively low-cost home with a majority of features found in today's high-priced homes. The three bedroom sleeping area highlights two full baths. The living area is a huge room of approximately 25 feet in depth zoned for both formal living and dining. The kitchen is extremely well-planned with even a built-in desk and pantry. The family room has a snack bar and sliding glass doors to the terrace. Blueprints include basement details.

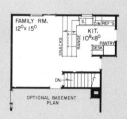

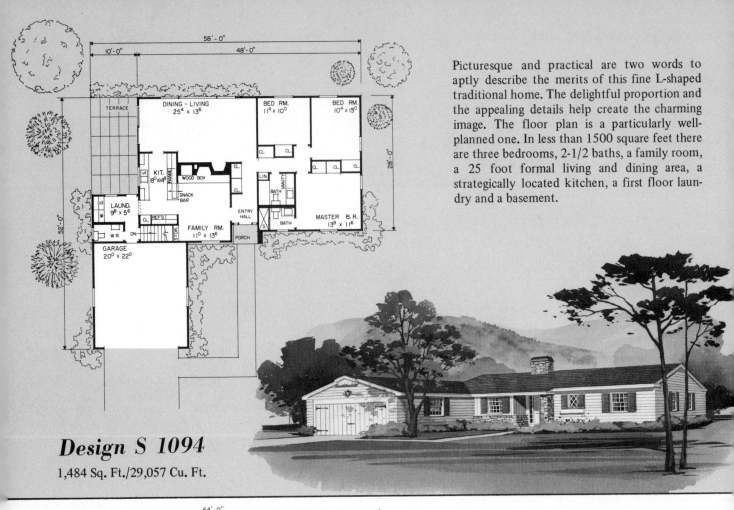

Picturesque and practical are two words to aptly describe the merits of this fine L-shaped traditional home. The delightful proportion and the appealing details help create the charming image. The floor plan is a particularly well-planned one. In less than 1500 square feet there are three bedrooms, 2-1/2 baths, a family room, a 25 foot formal living and dining area, a strategically located kitchen, a first floor laundry and a basement.

Design S 1094
1,484 Sq. Ft./29,057 Cu. Ft.

Charming, is but one of the many words that could be chosen to describe this traditional home. While essentially a frame house, the front exterior features natural quarried stone. Below the overhanging roof, the window and door treatment is most pleasing. The board fence, with its lamppost, completes a delightful picture. Highlighting the interior is the living room with its raised hearth fireplace.

Design S 1024
1,232 Sq. Ft./23,925 Cu. Ft.

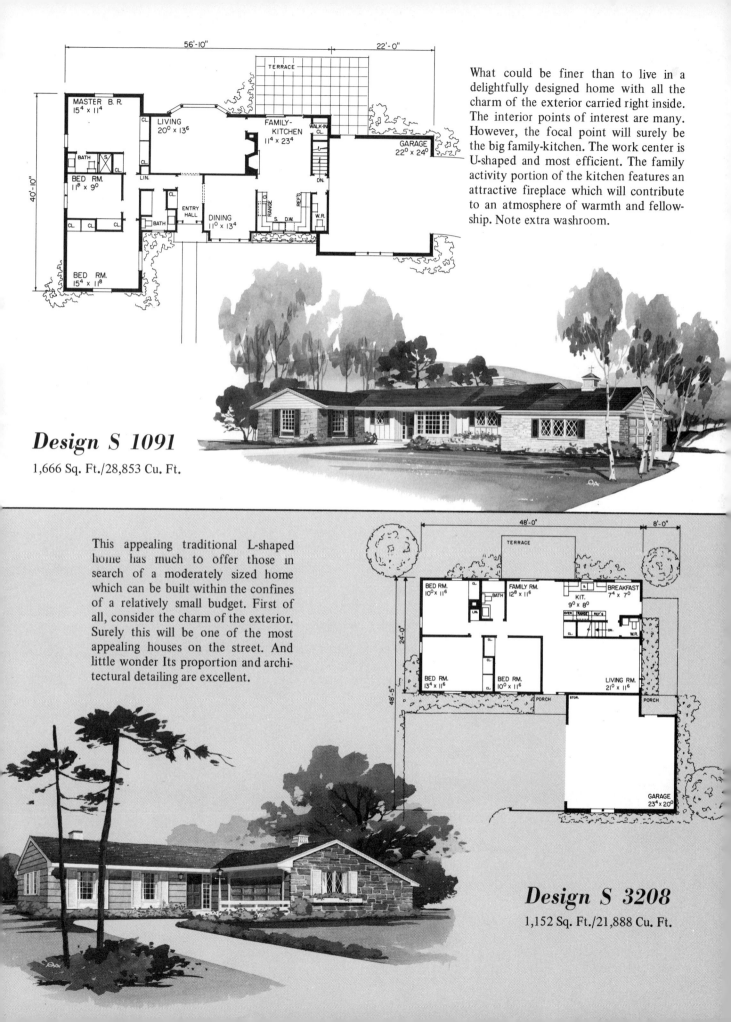

56'-10" **22'-0"**

TERRACE

MASTER B. R.
15⁴ x 11⁴

LIVING
20⁰ x 13⁶

FAMILY-
KITCHEN
11⁴ x 23⁴

WALK-IN
CL.

GARAGE
22⁰ x 24⁰

BATH

BED RM.
11⁸ x 9⁰

CL.

CL.

LIN.

CL.

DN.

40'-10"

CL. CL. CL.

ENTRY
HALL

BATH

DINING
11⁰ x 13⁴

RANGE

S. D.W.

REF.

W.R.

BED RM.
15⁴ x 11⁸

What could be finer than to live in a delightfully designed home with all the charm of the exterior carried right inside. The interior points of interest are many. However, the focal point will surely be the big family-kitchen. The work center is U-shaped and most efficient. The family activity portion of the kitchen features an attractive fireplace which will contribute to an atmosphere of warmth and fellowship. Note extra washroom.

Design S 1091
1,666 Sq. Ft./28,853 Cu. Ft.

This appealing traditional L-shaped home has much to offer those in search of a moderately sized home which can be built within the confines of a relatively small budget. First of all, consider the charm of the exterior. Surely this will be one of the most appealing houses on the street. And little wonder Its proportion and architectural detailing are excellent.

48'-0" **8'-0"**

TERRACE

BED RM.
10⁰ x 11⁶

FAMILY RM.
12⁸ x 11⁶

KIT.
9⁰ x 8⁰

BREAKFAST
7⁴ x 7⁰

BATH

LIN.

OVEN RANGE REF'S

CL.

DN.

W.R.

24'-0"

BED RM.
13⁴ x 11⁶

CL.

BED RM.
10⁰ x 11⁶

CL.

LIVING RM.
21⁰ x 11⁶

48'-5"

PORCH

STOR.

PORCH

GARAGE
23⁴ x 20⁰

Design S 3208
1,152 Sq. Ft./21,888 Cu. Ft.

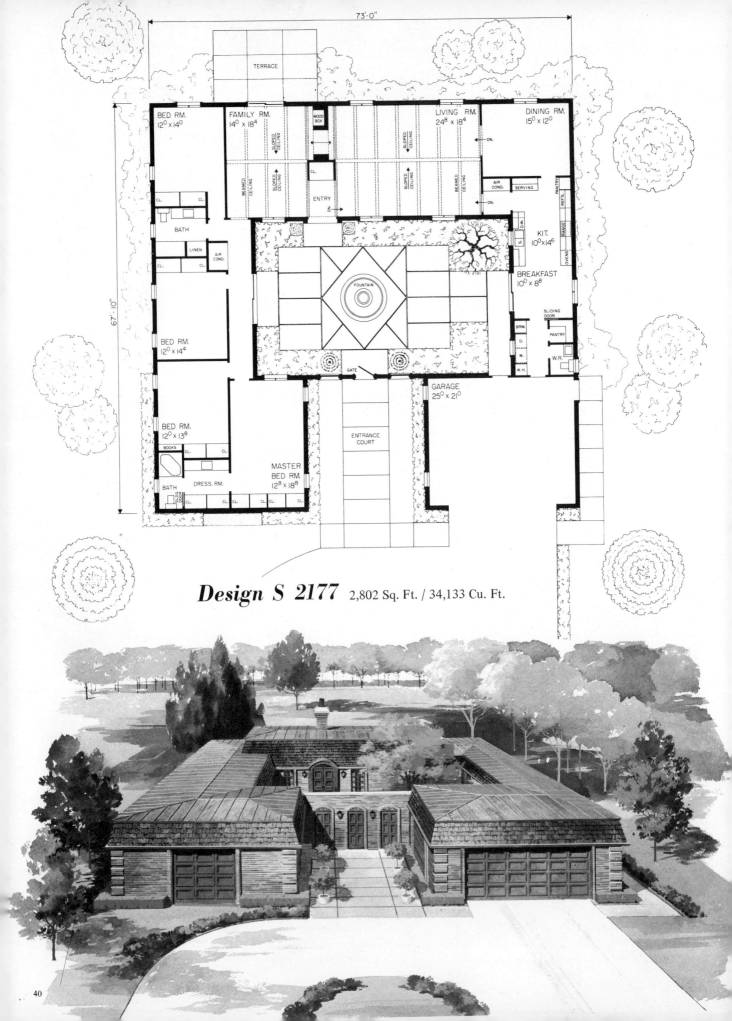

73'-0"

67'-10"

TERRACE

BED RM.
12⁰ x 14⁰

FAMILY RM.
14⁰ x 18⁴

WOOD
BOX

LIVING RM.
24⁸ x 18⁴

DINING RM.
15⁰ x 12⁰

SLOPED CEILING

BEAMED CEILING

SLOPED CEILING

SLOPED CEILING

SLOPED CEILING

BEAMED CEILING

ENTRY

DN.

DN.

DN.

CL.

CL.

CL.

BATH

AIR COND.

SERVING

PANTRY

REFG.

RANGE

LINEN

AIR COND.

D.W.

KIT.
10⁰ x 14⁶

CL.

CL.

OVENS

BED RM.
12⁰ x 14⁴

FOUNTAIN

BREAKFAST
10⁰ x 8⁸

SLIDING DOOR

BRM.

D.

PANTRY

W.

W.H.

W.R.

GATE

BED RM.
12⁰ x 13⁸

BOOKS

CL.

GARAGE
25⁰ x 21⁰

ENTRANCE
COURT

BATH

SLIDING DOOR

DRESS. RM.

MASTER
BED RM.
12⁸ x 18⁸

CL.

CL.

CL.

CL.

CL.

Design S 2177   2,802 Sq. Ft. / 34,133 Cu. Ft.

40

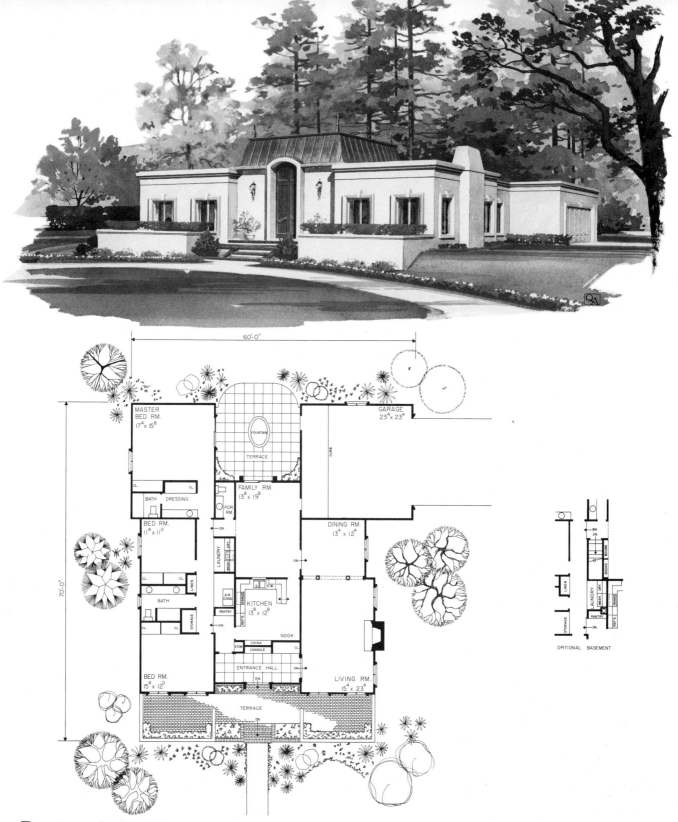

Design S 2347 2,322 Sq. Ft. / 26,572 Cu. Ft.

The regal character of this distinctive home is most inviting. The symmetry of the front exterior is enhanced by the raised terrace. The recessed front entrance shelters panelled double doors which open to the formal hall. Traffic may pass to the right directly into the sunken living room. To the left is the sunken three bedroom, two-bath sleeping area. The center of the plan features the efficient kitchen with nook space and the family room. The rear terrace, enclosed on three sides to assure privacy, is accessible from master bedroom, as well as family room, through sliding glass doors. Separating the formal living and dining rooms are finely proportioned, round wood columns. Don't overlook the first floor laundry. Blueprints include details for optional partial basement.

Design S 2220

2,646 Sq. Ft./35,392 Cu. Ft.

The gracious formality of this home is reminiscent of a popularly accepted French styling. The hip-roof, the brick quoins, the cornice details, the arched window heads, the distinctive shutters, the recessed double front doors, the massive center chimney, and the delightful flower court are all features which set the dramatic appeal of this home. This floor plan is a favorite of many. The four bedroom, two bath sleeping wing is a zone by itself. Further, the formal living and dining rooms are ideally located.

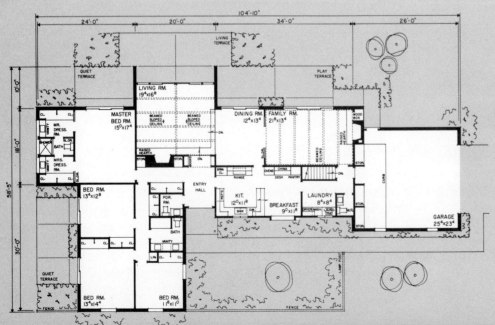

For country-estate living. This L-shaped traditional home will be a worthy addition to any building site. Its pleasing proportions are almost breath-taking and seem to foretell the tremendous amount of livability its inhabitants are sure to enjoy. The zoning for pleasurable living could hardly be improved upon. The children's bedrooms function together in a wing with its own bath. The large master bedroom has separate "Mr." and "Mrs." dressing rooms flanking a common bath. The living room is sunken and but a step from the terrace.

Design S 1892

1,986 Sq. Ft./26,340 Cu. Ft.

The romance of French Provincial is captured here by the hip-roof masses, the charm of the window detailing, the brick quoins at the corners, the delicate dentil work at the cornices, the massive centered chimney, and the recessed double front doors. The slightly raised entry court completes the picture. The basic floor plan is a favorite of many. And little wonder, for all areas work well together, while still maintaining a fine degree of separation of functions. The highlight of the interior will be the sunken living room.

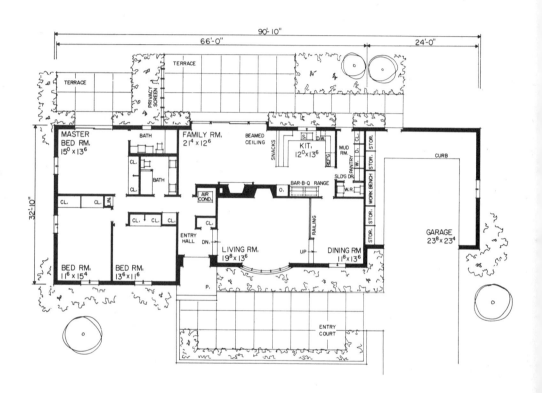

Design S 1952

2,705 Sq. Ft./41,582 Cu. Ft.

Design S 1191
1,232 Sq. Ft./15,400 Cu. Ft.

A careful study of the floor plan for this cozy appearing traditional home reveals a fine combination of features which add tremendously to convenient living. For instance, observe the wardrobe and storage facilities of the bedroom area. Then, notice the economical plumbing of the two back-to-back baths. Further, don't overlook the locations of the washer and dryer which have cupboards above the units themselves. Observe storage facilities.

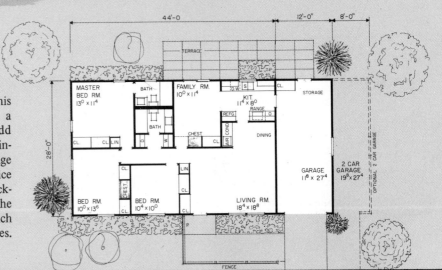

Design S 1939
1,387 Sq. Ft./28,000 Cu. Ft.

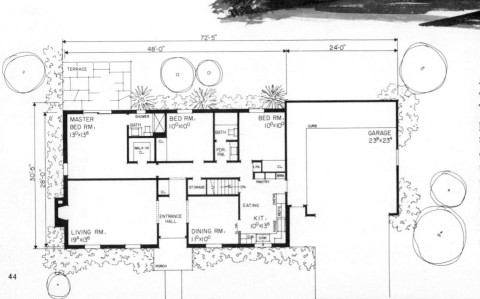

A delightfully proportioned house with more than its full share of charm. The brick veneer exterior contrasts pleasingly with the narrow horizontal siding of the oversized attached two-car garage. Perhaps the focal point of the exterior is the recessed front entrance with its double Colonial styled doors. The secondary service entrance through the garage to the kitchen area is a handy feature. The pantry units are strategically located as are the stairs to the basement.

Delightful design and effective, flexible planning come in little packages, too. This fine traditional exterior with its covered front entrance features an alternate basement plan. Note how the non-basement layout provides a family room and mud room, while the basement option shows kitchen eating and dining room.

OPTIONAL BASEMENT PLAN

Design S 1311
1,050 Sq. Ft./11,370 Cu. Ft.

Design S 1075
1,232 Sq. Ft./24,123 Cu. Ft.

This picturesque traditional one-story home has much to offer the young family. Because of its rectangular shape and its predominantly frame exterior, construction costs will be economical. Passing through the front entrance, visitors will be surprised to find so much livability in only 1232 square feet. Consider these features: spacious formal living and dining area; two full baths; efficient kitchen; large rear family room. In addition, there is the full basement for further recreational facilities and storage.

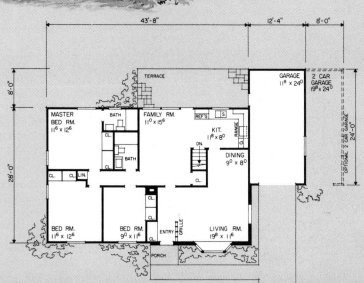

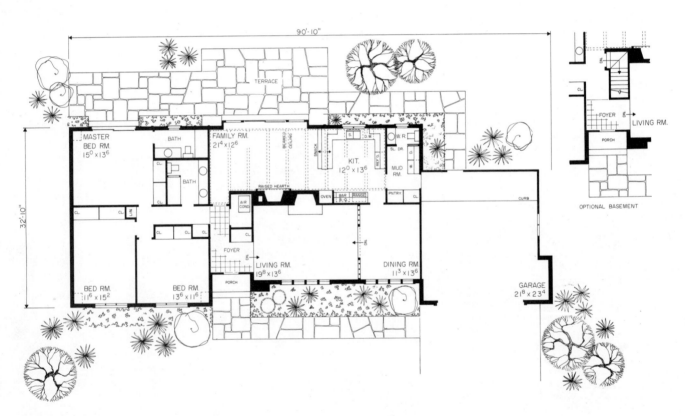

TERRACE

MASTER BED RM. 15⁰ x 13⁶

BATH

BATH

FAMILY RM. 21⁴ x 12⁶

BEAMED CEILING

SNACK

KIT. 12⁰ x 13⁶

REF'G.

SL. DR.

W.R.

MUD RM.

PNTRY

CL

RAISED HEARTH

OVEN

BAR 8'-9"

RANGE

AIR COND.

CL

CL

CL

CL

LIN

CL

FOYER

LIVING RM. 19⁸ x 13⁶

DINING RM. 11³ x 13⁶

CURB

PORCH

BED RM. 11⁶ x 15²

BED RM. 13⁶ x 11⁶

90'-10"

32'-10"

GARAGE 21⁸ x 23⁴

FOYER

LIVING RM.

PORCH

OPTIONAL BASEMENT

Design S 2318 2,029 Sq. Ft. / 31,021 Cu. Ft.

Warmth and charm are characteristics of the Tudor adaptations. This modest sized home, with its twin front-facing gabled roofs, represents a great investment. While it will be an exciting and refreshing addition to any neighborhood, its appeal will never grow old.

The covered front entrance opens to the center foyer. Traffic patterns flow in an orderly and efficient manner to the three main zones - the formal dining zone, the sleeping zone, and the informal living zone. The sunken living room with its fireplace is separated

from the dining room by an attractive trellis divider. A second fireplace along with beamed ceiling and sliding glass doors highlight the family room. Note snack bar, mud room, cooking facilities, two full baths and optional basement for more storage and rec space.

Design S 2515 2,363 Sq. Ft. / 46,676 Cu. Ft.

Another Tudor adaptation with all the appeal that is inherent in this design style. The brick veneer exterior is effectively complimented by the beam work, the stucco, and the window treatment. The carriage lamp perched on the planter wall adds a delightful touch as do the dovecotes of the bedroom wing and over the garage door. The livability of the interior is just great. The kitchen, nook, and dining room overlook the front yard. Around the corner from the kitchen is the laundry with an extra wash room not far away. Sloping, beamed ceiling and raised hearth fireplace are highlights of the family room. Like the living room and master bedroom it functions with rear terrace. Note vanity outside main bath. Stolid wood posts on 3 foot wall separate living room and hall.

This convenient living design features a sleeping zone comprised of three bedrooms and two full baths; a formal living zone made up of a sunken living room, and a separate dining room; an informal living zone highlighting a family room and a spacious U-shaped kitchen.

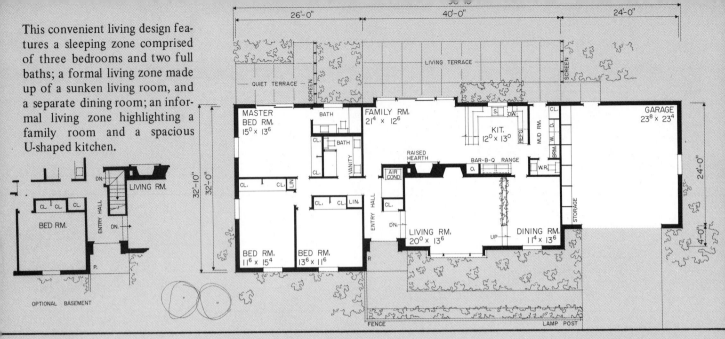

Design S 1325

1,942 Sq. Ft./35,384 Cu. Ft.

Unless your visitors arrive by plane they will not get this birds-eye view of your new home. However, they will be no less impressed as they swing their car into your driveway. Their attention will focus on the inviting recessed front entrance with its double doors. The large front entry hall permits direct access to the formal living room, the sleeping area, and the informal family room. When formal dining is the occasion of the evening the separate dining room is but a step from the living room.

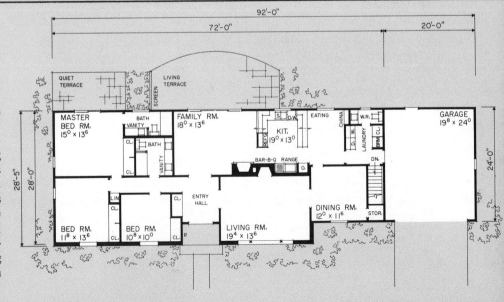

Design S 1748

1,986 Sq. Ft./23,311 Cu. Ft.

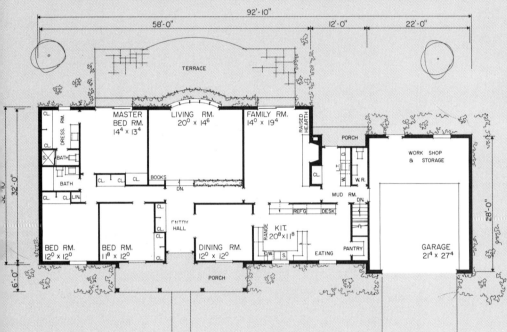

Design S 1788

2,218 Sq. Ft./36,002 Cu. Ft.

Charm, is but one of many words which may be used to correctly describe this fine design. In addition to its eye-appeal, it has a practical and smoothly functioning floor plan. The detail of the front entrance, highlighted by columns supporting the projecting pediment gable, is outstanding. Observe the window treatment and the double front doors. Perhaps the focal point of the interior will be the formal living room. It is, indeed, dramatic. Note mud room area.

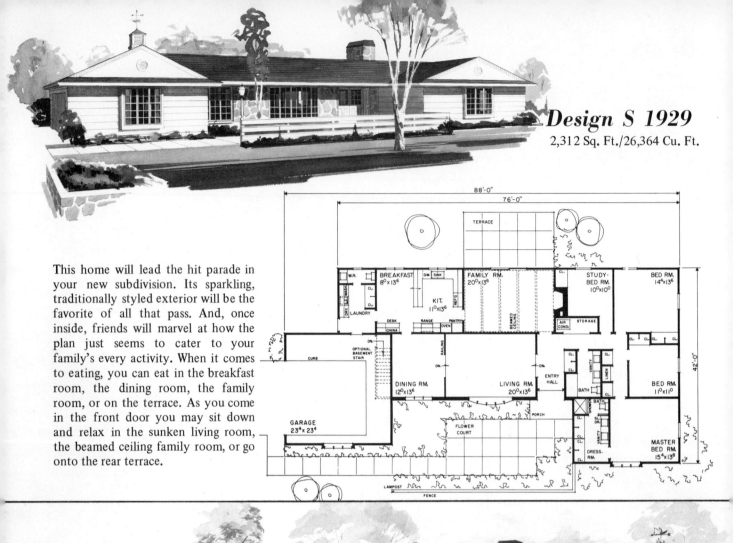

Design S 1929

2,312 Sq. Ft./26,364 Cu. Ft.

This home will lead the hit parade in your new subdivision. Its sparkling, traditionally styled exterior will be the favorite of all that pass. And, once inside, friends will marvel at how the plan just seems to cater to your family's every activity. When it comes to eating, you can eat in the breakfast room, the dining room, the family room, or on the terrace. As you come in the front door you may sit down and relax in the sunken living room, the beamed ceiling family room, or go onto the rear terrace.

Design S 1835

2,144 Sq. Ft./33,310 Cu. Ft.

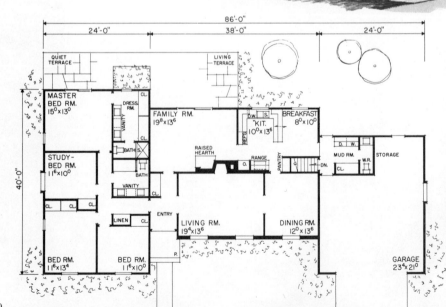

Cedar shakes and quarried natural stone, are the exterior materials which adorn this irregularly shaped traditional ranch home. Adding to the appeal of the exterior are the cut-up windows, the shutters, the pediment gable, the cupola, and the double front doors. The detail of the garage door opening adds further interest. Inside, this favorite among floor plans, reflects all the features necessary to provide complete livability for the large family. The sleeping zone is a 24' x 40' rectangle which contains four bedrooms and two full baths.

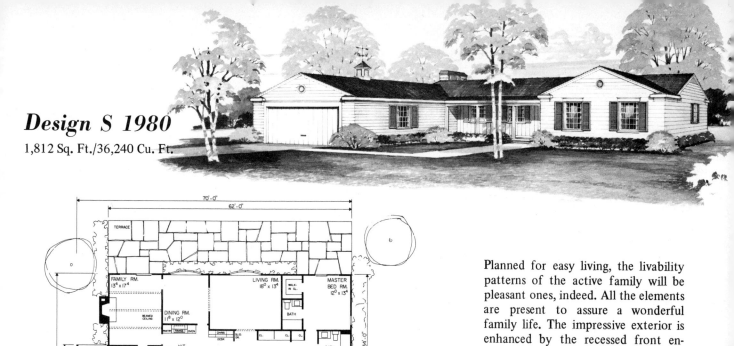

Design S 1980
1,812 Sq. Ft./36,240 Cu. Ft.

Planned for easy living, the livability patterns of the active family will be pleasant ones, indeed. All the elements are present to assure a wonderful family life. The impressive exterior is enhanced by the recessed front entrance area with its covered porch. The center entry results in a convenient and efficient flow of traffic. A secondary entrance leads from the garage, or covered side porch, into the first floor laundry. With the powder room nearby, this will be an ideal mud room.

Design S 1829
1,800 Sq. Ft./32,236 Cu. Ft.

All the charm of a traditional heritage is wrapped up in this U-shaped home with its narrow, horizontal siding, delightful window treatment, and high pitched roof. The massive center chimney, the bay window, and the double front doors are plus features. Inside, the living potential is outstanding. The sleeping wing is self-contained and has four bedrooms and two baths. The large family and living rooms permit divergent age groups in the family to enjoy themselves to the fullest.

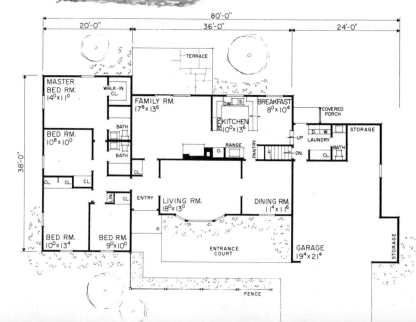

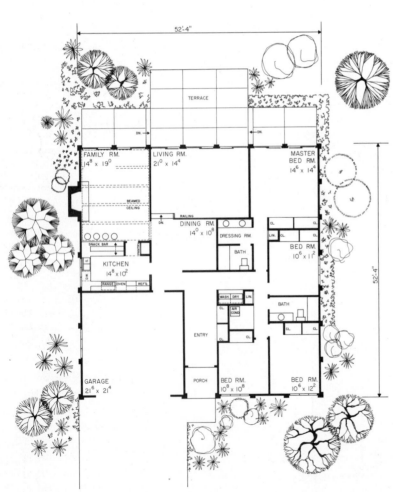

Design S 2357

2,135 Sq. Ft. / 24,970 Cu. Ft.

Palm trees on your site are not a prerequisite for the building of this distinctive home. If you and your family have a flair for things unique, the exterior, as well as the interior, of this attractive design will excite you. The low-pitched, wide overhanging hip roof has a slag surface. The equally spaced pillars and the spaces between the vertical boards are finished in stucco. This house is a perfect square measuring 52'-4". The resulting plan is one that is practical and efficient. The kitchen will be a joy in which to work. A pass-thru provides the access to the snack bar of the beamed ceilinged family room. The formal dining area is but a couple steps away and overlooks the sunken living room. Four bedrooms and two baths make up the sleeping zone.

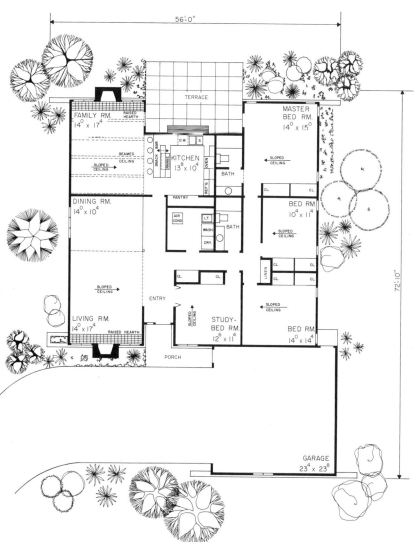

Design S 2348

2,067 Sq. Ft. / 23,068 Cu. Ft.

Contemporary design and planning can take many shapes. This house ably attests to what interesting shapes and fine living patterns can result. The varying roof planes and the brick masses help set the character. The recessed front door opens to the entry which leads straight to the kitchen at the rear of plan. The living and dining rooms have sloped ceilings and are openly planned for a fine feeling of spaciousness. The sloping, beamed ceiling family room functions well with the efficient kitchen. There is a snack bar and access to the terrace. Each living area has a dramatic raised hearth fireplace. For sleeping facilities there are four bedrooms and two baths. Note how the terrace is accessible from the master bedroom. That is a serving counter on the terrace just below the kitchen window.

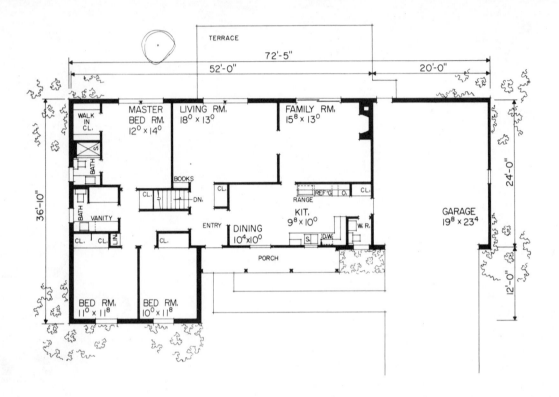

Floor plan labels:

TERRACE

72'-5"

52'-0"   20'-0"

WALK IN CL.

MASTER BED RM. 12⁰ x 14⁰

LIVING RM. 18⁰ x 13⁰

FAMILY RM. 15⁸ x 13⁰

24'-0"

BATH S.

BOOKS

REF'G O. CL.
RANGE

36'-10"

BATH

CL. DN.

GARAGE 19⁸ x 23⁴

VANITY

KIT. 9⁸ x 10⁰

12'-0"

CL. CL. LIN.

CL.

ENTRY DINING 10⁴ x 10⁰

S. D.W.

W.R.

BED RM. 11⁰ x 11⁸

BED RM. 10⁰ x 11⁸

PORCH

Design S 1716   1,560 Sq. Ft./28,860 Cu. Ft.

Here is the American ranch style at its best. The simplicity of its exterior materials — brick veneer and horizontal wood siding — sets off the elegance of the deep windows and shutters. The covered porch with its wood pillars contribute an extra measure of charm.

Inside, the plan provides an excellent pattern for circulation. The attached two-car garage results in a short, dry walk to the kitchen when toting groceries from car to cabinet. The strategically located half-bath doubles as a mud room. The kitchen offers a large

area for dining. On special occasions the family room with its fireplace could function as a delightful, formal dining area. The living room may be completely by-passed. Blueprints for this particular design include all optional elevations.

Design S 1321 1,478 Sq. Ft./30,447 Cu. Ft.

Design S 1320 1,478 Sq. Ft./27,195 Cu. Ft.

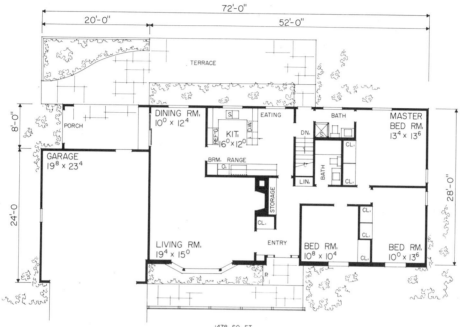

A delightful design series with a practical and efficient floor plan. Each exterior has a separate set of blueprints. The center entrance routes traffic effectively. Each of the three bedrooms is of good size. The master bedroom has direct access to one of the two baths which is also ideally located in relation to the rear yard, the kitchen area, and the basement stairs. The hall area features a wardrobe closet, a long miscellaneous storage unit, and a handy linen closet. The spaciousness of open planning is exemplified by the arrangement of the formal living and dining areas. The bay window, the fireplace, the long blank wall, and the glass sliding doors to the covered porch are highlights. Don't miss the kitchen eating space and the convenient pass-thru.

Design S 1322 1,478 Sq. Ft./28,969 Cu. Ft.

Design S 1938 1,428 Sq. Ft./29,702 Cu. Ft.

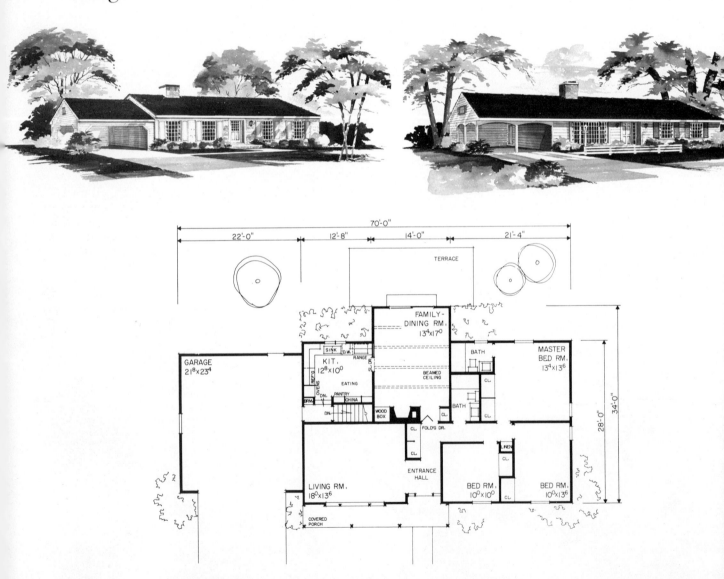

A fine efficient plan designed to fit each of the three delightful exteriors above. You can reserve your choice of exterior until you receive the blueprints. Each set you order contains the details for the construction of all three. Note the differences in exterior materials, window treatment, car storage facilities, and roof lines. Observe the beamed ceiling, all-purpose family room and the kitchen eating space.

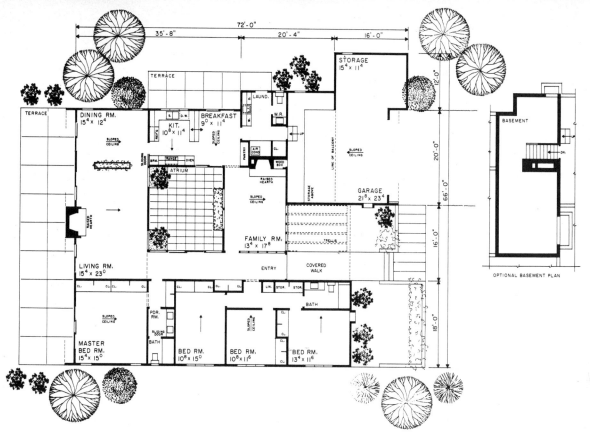

Design S 2135   2,495 Sq. Ft. — Excluding Atrium/28,928 Cu. Ft.

For those seeking a new experience in home ownership. The proud occupants of this contemporary home will forever be thrilled at their choice of such a distinguished exterior and such a practical and exciting floor plan. The variety of shed roof planes contrast dramatically with the simplicity of the vertical siding. Inside there is a feeling of spaciousness resulting from the sloping ceilings. The uniqueness of this design is further enhanced by the atrium. Open to the sky, this outdoor area, indoors, can be enjoyed from all parts of the house. The sleeping zone has four bedrooms, two baths, and plenty of closets. The informal living zone has a fine kitchen, breakfast room, and family room. For formal living there is the spacious living and dining area. Note bulk storage room.

Design S 1891

1,986 Sq. Ft./23,022 Cu. Ft.

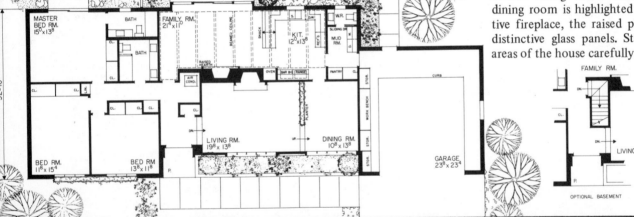

There is much more to a house than just its exterior. And while the appeal of this home would be difficult to beat, it is the living potential of the interior that gives this design such a high ranking. The sunken living room with its adjacent dining room is highlighted by the attractive fireplace, the raised planter and the distinctive glass panels. Study the other areas of the house carefully.

OPTIONAL BASEMENT

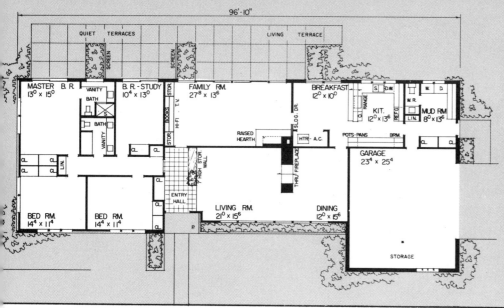

Design S 1023
2,624 Sq. Ft./27,556 Cu. Ft.

Features galore, and ones that will be sure to help guarantee years of convenient living. Starting with the sleeping zone, there are four bedrooms, two baths with built-in vanities, and plenty of closets. The delightfully large living areas occupy the center of the plan. Overlooking the front yard through a dramatic bank of windows is the formal area for living and dining. An attractive through fireplace acts as the practical room divider.

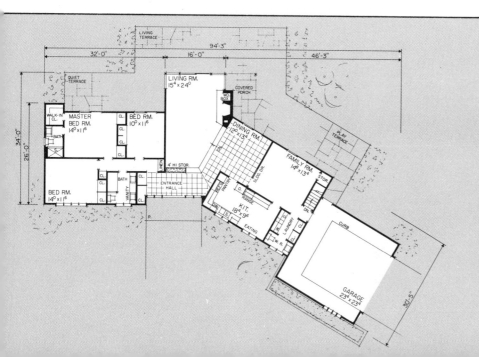

Design S 1884
1,925 Sq. Ft./26,062 Cu. Ft.

If you are searching for something with an air of distinction both inside and out then search no more. You could hardly improve upon what this home has to offer. You will forever be proud of the impressive hip-roof, angular facade. Its interest will give it an identity all its own. As for the interior, your everyday living patterns will be a delight, indeed. And little wonder, for clever zoning and a fine feeling of spaciousness set the stage.

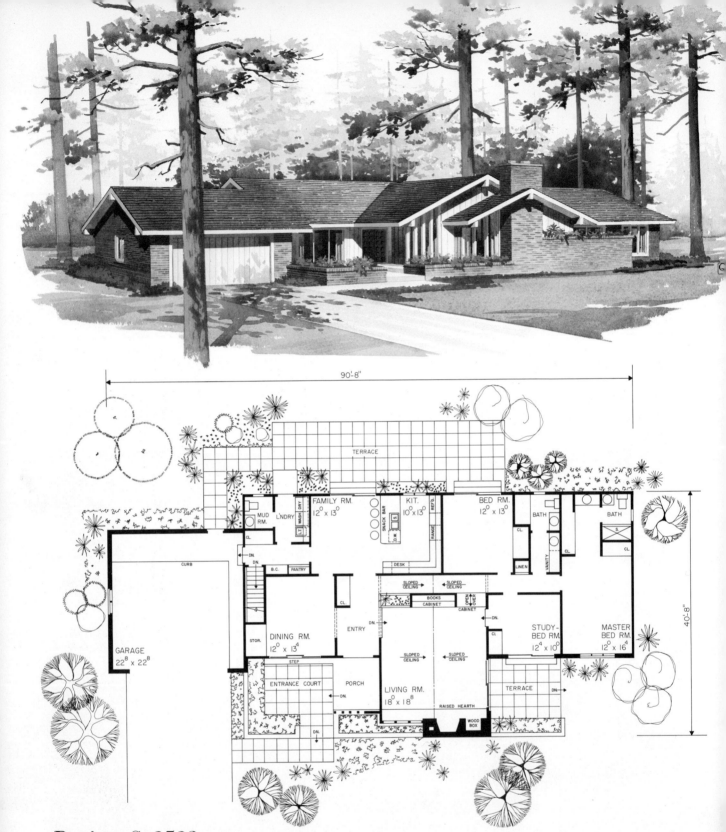

TERRACE

FAMILY RM.
12⁰ x 13⁰

KIT.
10⁰ x 13⁰

BED RM.
12⁰ x 13⁰

MUD RM.

L'NDRY

WASH DRY

SNACK BAR

D.W.

REF'S

RANGE

BATH

BATH

CL.

CL.

LINEN

VANITY

CL.

S

CL.

DESK

CURB

DN.

DN.

B.C.

PANTRY

CL.

SLOPED CEILING

SLOPED CEILING

BOOKS CABINET

OPEN OVER CABINET

DN.

CL.

GARAGE
22⁸ x 22⁸

STOR.

DINING RM.
12⁰ x 13⁴

ENTRY

DN.

STUDY-BED RM.
12⁴ x 10⁰

MASTER BED RM.
12⁰ x 16⁴

SLOPED CEILING

SLOPED CEILING

STEP

ENTRANCE COURT

PORCH

LIVING RM.
18⁰ x 18⁸

TERRACE

DN.

DN.

RAISED HEARTH

WOOD BOX

90'-8"

40'-8"

Design S 2523 2,055 Sq. Ft. / 43,702 Cu. Ft.

You'll want the investment in your new home to be one of the soundest you'll ever make. And certainly the best way to do this is to make sure your new home has unexcelled exterior appeal and outstanding interior livability. For those who like refreshing contemporary lines, this design will rate at the top. The wide overhanging roof, the brick masses, the glass areas, the raised planters, and the covered front entrance highlight the facade. As for the interior, all the elements are present to assure fine living patterns. Consider the room relationships and how they function with one another. Note how they relate to the outdoors. Be sure to list all the features which appeal to you and your family the most. Observe that the living room is sunken one step.

Design S 2343   3,110 Sq. Ft. / 51,758 Cu. Ft.

If yours is a growing and active family the chances are good that they will want their new home to relate to the outdoors. This distinctive design puts a premium on private outdoor living. And you don't have to install a swim-ming pool to get the most enjoyment from this home. Developing this area as a garden court will provide the in-door living areas with a breath-taking awareness of nature's beauty. Notice the fine zoning of the plan and how each area has its sliding glass doors to provide an unrestricted view. Three bedrooms plus study are serviced by three baths. The family and gathering rooms provide two great living areas. The kitchen is most efficient.

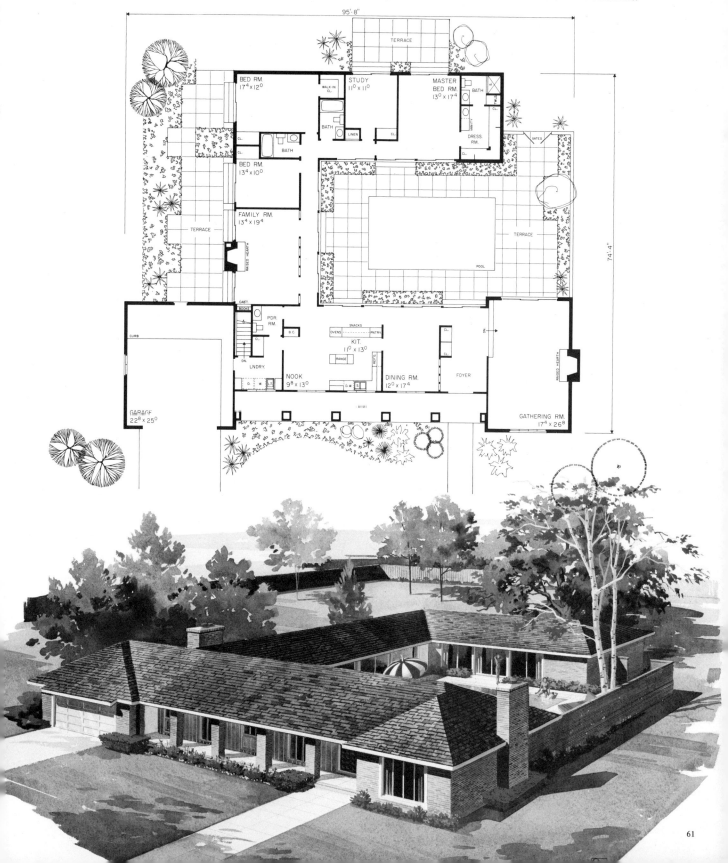

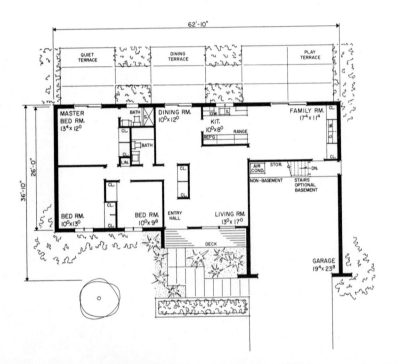

Design S 1383
1,382 Sq. Ft./15,448 Cu. Ft.

An appealing contemporary highlighted by a low-pitched, wide-overhanging roof. Brick is the dominant exterior material with a modest use of horizontal siding adding to the appeal. The window treatment is pleasingly simple. Double front doors open into the center entry hall. The kitchen is strategically located between the formal dining room and the informal family room. Each of these three rooms has a view of the rear yard. Sliding glass doors provide the family room with direct access to the terrace. Don't miss the storage facilities and the stall shower of the master bath. Blueprints include optional basement details.

Design S 1342 1,560 Sq. Ft./13,256 Cu. Ft.

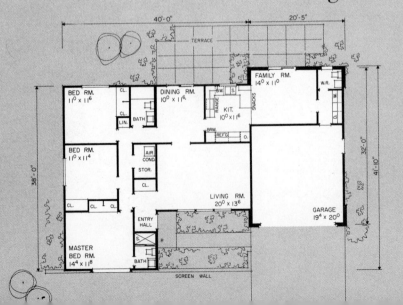

A well-planned, medium sized contemporary home with plenty of big-house features. The brick line of the projected bedroom wing extends toward the projected two-car garage to form an attractive front court. The large glass panels below the overhanging roof are a dramatic feature. In addition to the two full baths, there is an extra wash room easily accessible from the kitchen/family room area as well as the outdoors. The laundry equipment is strategically located.

Design S 1307

1,357 Sq. Ft./14,476 Cu. Ft.

The popularity of this home is easy to understand. Its pleasingly contemporary exterior has simple lines. Its L shape permits orientation on the site with either the garage door, or the front door, facing the street. Inside, traffic moves efficiently between the three distinct zones — the sleeping zone, the formal living and dining area, and the informal family room/kitchen zone. Adjacent to the family room is the laundry area.

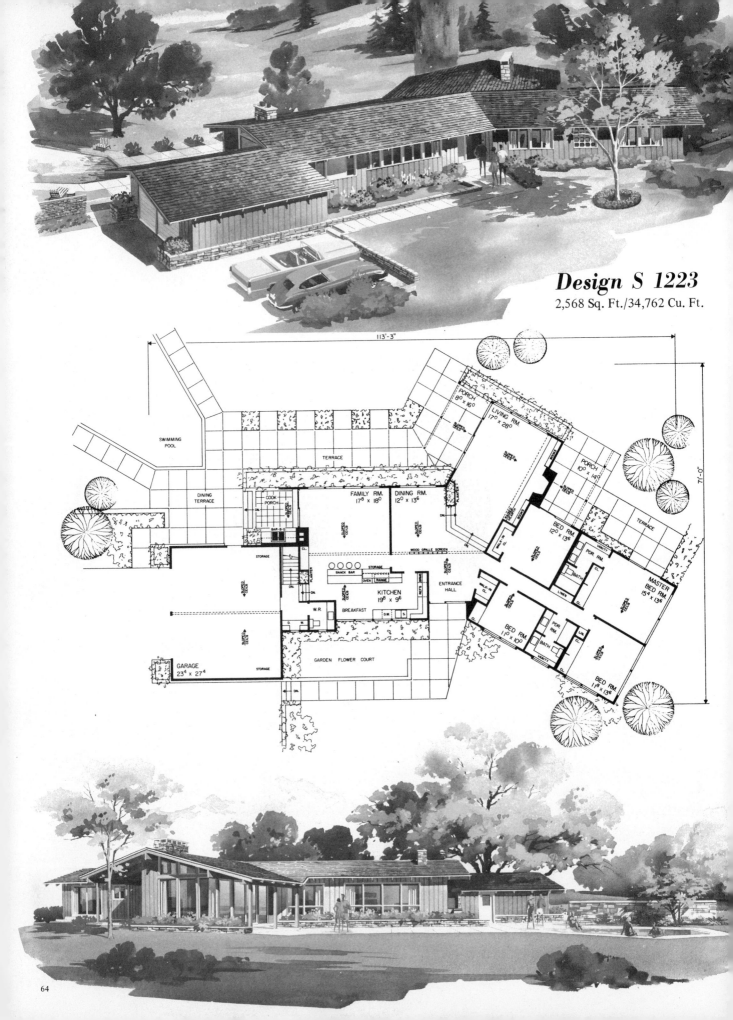

Design S 1223

2,568 Sq. Ft./34,762 Cu. Ft.

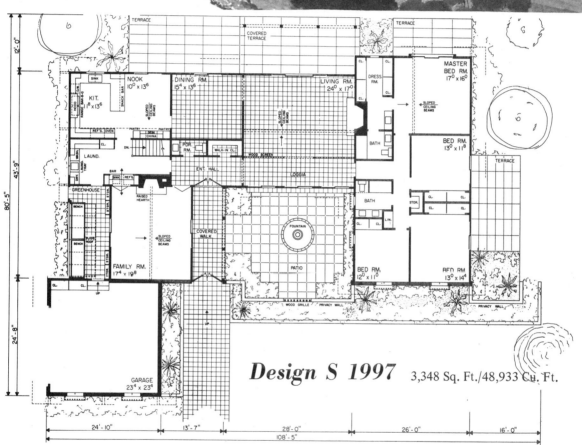

Design S 1997 3,348 Sq. Ft./48,933 Cu. Ft.

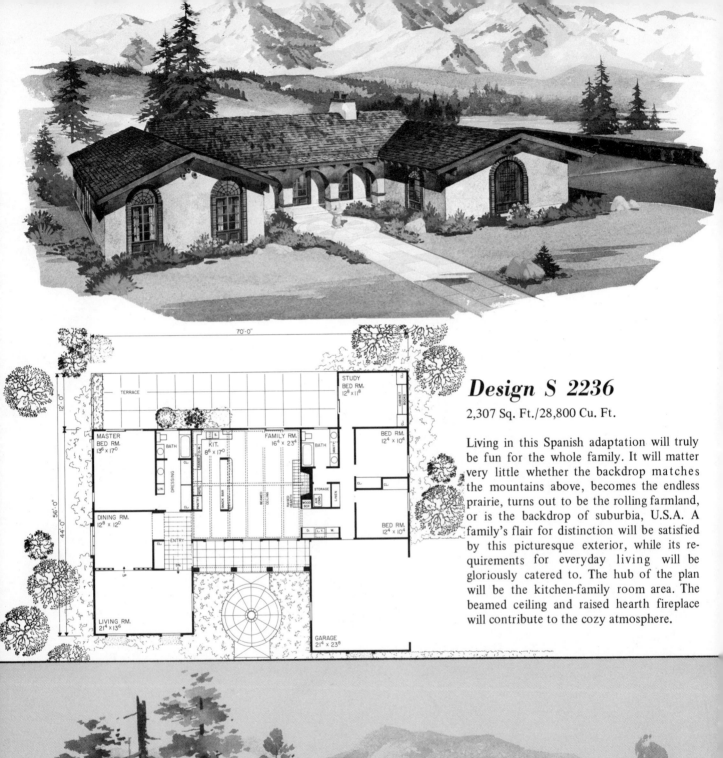

Design S 2236

2,307 Sq. Ft./28,800 Cu. Ft.

Living in this Spanish adaptation will truly be fun for the whole family. It will matter very little whether the backdrop matches the mountains above, becomes the endless prairie, turns out to be the rolling farmland, or is the backdrop of suburbia, U.S.A. A family's flair for distinction will be satisfied by this picturesque exterior, while its requirements for everyday living will be gloriously catered to. The hub of the plan will be the kitchen-family room area. The beamed ceiling and raised hearth fireplace will contribute to the cozy atmosphere.

Design S 1726

1,910 Sq. Ft./19,264 Cu. Ft.

The U-shaped plan has long been honored for its excellent zoning. As the plan for this fine Spanish adaptation illustrates, it not only provides separation between parents' area and children's wing, but also places a buffer area in the center. This makes the kitchen the "control center" for the home — handy to the family room, living room, dining alcove. Take another look at the dining space. There's a special treat here with floor-to-ceiling windows on the three sides. Can you imagine a more cheerful spot in which to dine?

Design S 2200

1,695 Sq. Ft./18,916 Cu. Ft.

If you have a penchant for something delightfully different, then this Spanish adaptation may be just what you've been waiting for. This L-shaped ranch home will go well on any site — large or small. A popular feature will be the atrium. Of great interest are the indoor-outdoor relationships. Observe how the major rooms function through sliding glass doors with the terraces. The interior has a feeling of spaciousness with a number of large glass areas and sloping ceilings. The open planning of the living area will be enjoyable, indeed.

Design S 2266 2,668 Sq. Ft./38,926 Cu. Ft.

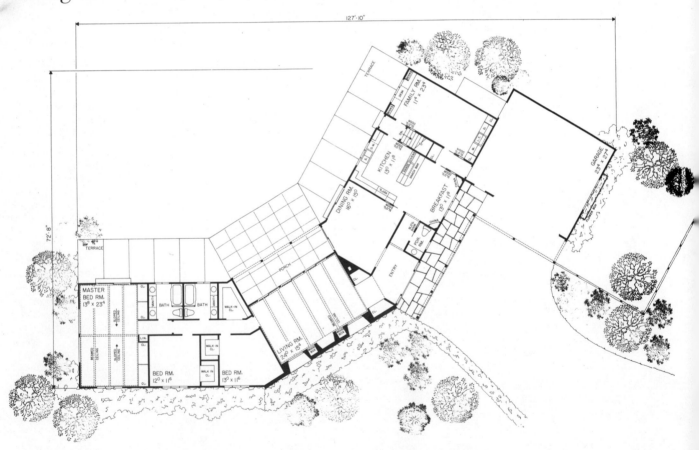

Westward Ho! Here's a plan that will stir your imagination. If you desire to provide your family with living patterns that will be a refreshing break with convention, this interesting design may just fit the bill. Certainly the exterior will satisfy your predilection for something distinctive in your next home. The wide overhanging roof with its exposed rafter tails, the massive chimney, the covered front porch, the deeply recessed windows, and the spacious drive court are wonderfully appealing features. Inside the double front doors is the spacious entry which routes traffic to the formal and informal areas. Acting as a buffer for the sleeping wing is the beamed ceilinged living room. Sliding glass doors permit this fine room to function with the covered rear porch. Study remainder of plan carefully. Noteworthy are the fine kitchen, snack bar, and breakfast room.

Design S 2258   2,504 Sq. Ft. / 26,292 Cu. Ft.

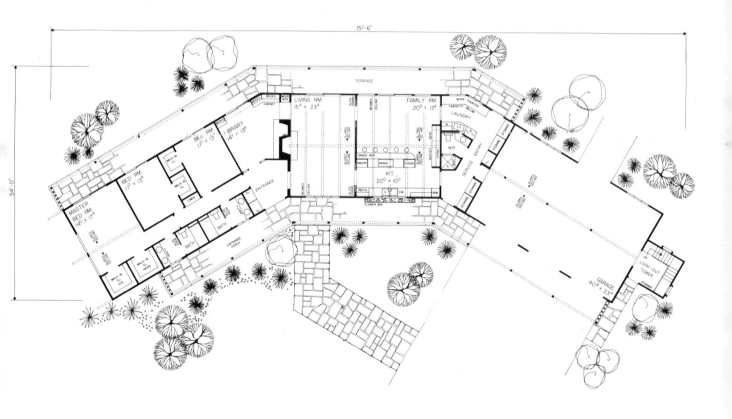

Here's a real Western Ranch House with all the appeal of its forebears. As for the livability offered by this angular design, the old days of the rugged west never had anything like this. Consider: A sleeping wing with three big bedrooms, walk-in closets, two compartmented baths; A library with raised hearth fireplace, built-in book shelves and cabinets; A spacious, sloping beamed ceilinged living room with fireplace; A family-kitchen area with snack bar, built-in buffet, desk, etc; A big service area with plenty of storage, wash room, complete laundry; A three car garage with sloped ceiling and an attached look-out tower. The front porch is, indeed, a delightful feature. The covered rear terrace runs the length of the house and is accessible through sliding glass doors.

Design S 2251

3,112 Sq. Ft./36,453 Cu. Ft.

103'-10"

78'-10"

POOL

BED RM.
$12^6 \times 13^0$

BED RM.
$12^6 \times 17^0$

WALK-IN
CL.

BATH

VANITY

LAUNDRY

CL.

LIN.

CL.

CL.

CL.

CL.

TERRACE

DN.

TERRACE

FAMILY RM.
$24^0 \times 19^6$

BED RM.
$12^6 \times 12^0$

KIT.
$12^0 \times 13^0$

SNACK BAR

DW.

S.

DINING RM.
$12^0 \times 13^0$

DN.

LIVING RM.
$23^4 \times 19^6$

CABINET

BOOKS

OVENS

B-B-Q

RANGE

PANTRY

ENTRANCE HALL

DN.

CABINET

BOOKS

UP

CL.

CL.

CL.

GARAGE
$27^4 \times 23^4$

DN.

UP

SER.
ENT.

CL.

WALK-IN
CL.

CHEST

BATH

SLID.
DOOR

BIDET

DN.

CHEST

CHEST

TERRACE

UP

MASTER
BED RM.
$23^4 \times 15^0$

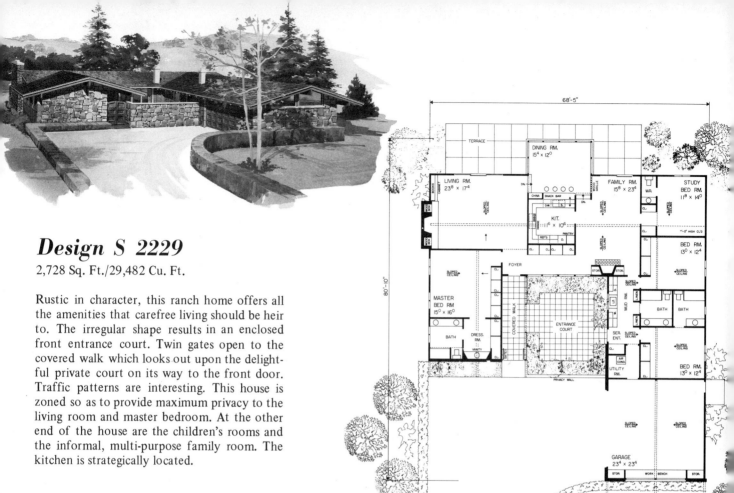

Design S 2229

2,728 Sq. Ft./29,482 Cu. Ft.

Rustic in character, this ranch home offers all the amenities that carefree living should be heir to. The irregular shape results in an enclosed front entrance court. Twin gates open to the covered walk which looks out upon the delightful private court on its way to the front door. Traffic patterns are interesting. This house is zoned so as to provide maximum privacy to the living room and master bedroom. At the other end of the house are the children's rooms and the informal, multi-purpose family room. The kitchen is strategically located.

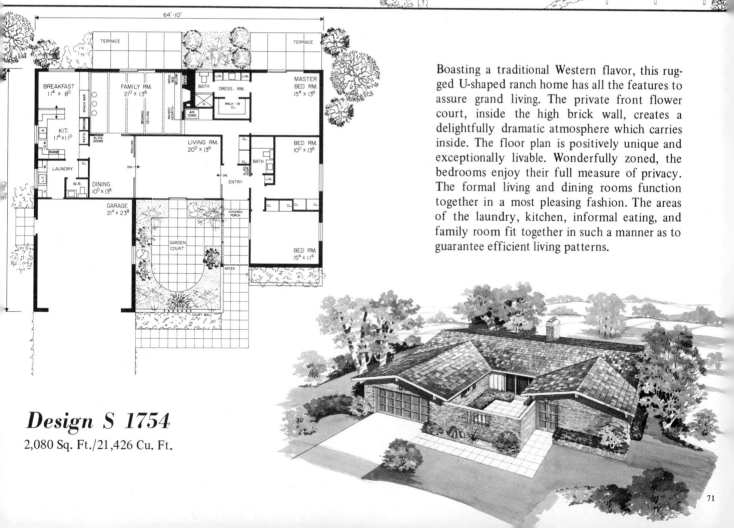

Boasting a traditional Western flavor, this rugged U-shaped ranch home has all the features to assure grand living. The private front flower court, inside the high brick wall, creates a delightfully dramatic atmosphere which carries inside. The floor plan is positively unique and exceptionally livable. Wonderfully zoned, the bedrooms enjoy their full measure of privacy. The formal living and dining rooms function together in a most pleasing fashion. The areas of the laundry, kitchen, informal eating, and family room fit together in such a manner as to guarantee efficient living patterns.

Design S 1754

2,080 Sq. Ft./21,426 Cu. Ft.

English Country House With Spacious Family Living

Design S 2245   2,855 Sq. Ft. — First Floor/955 Sq. Ft. — Second Floor/57,645 Cu. Ft.

The graciousness of this impressive English country house will endure for generations. The fine proportions, the exquisite architectural detailing, and the interesting configuration are among the elements that create such an overwhelming measure of true char-acter. Notice the natural quarried stone and the wavy siding. Observe the delicate treatment of the windows and the doors. The curving drive court adds to the feeling of grandeur. The cupola, the twin stone chimneys with their pots, and the carriage lamps are pleasing features. The garden view shows the three spacious outdoor ter-race areas. Notice the box bay win-dows and both the front and rear dormers. Whatever the setting, this family home will be one of the domi-nant features of the countryside.

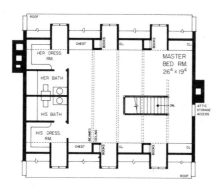

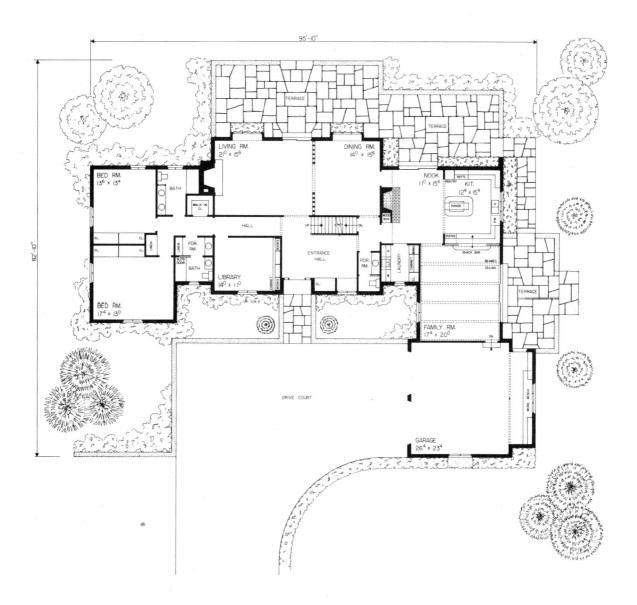

The interior of this home will be as dramatic as the exterior. The recessed front entrance opens into a spacious, formal entrance hall. From here traffic patterns flow efficiently to all areas of the house. Around the corner is the hall leading to the big library and the two children's rooms. Two full baths service this area. Straight ahead is the formal living room with its overview of, and access to, the rear yard. An appealing traditionally styled divider with raised panel moldings, turned spindles and a massive wood beam separates the living and dining rooms. To the right, the large kitchen area, with its eating space and fireplace, enjoys a warm country kitchen atmosphere. Beamed ceilings, snack bar, and sliding glass doors are family room highlights. Notice garage work area.

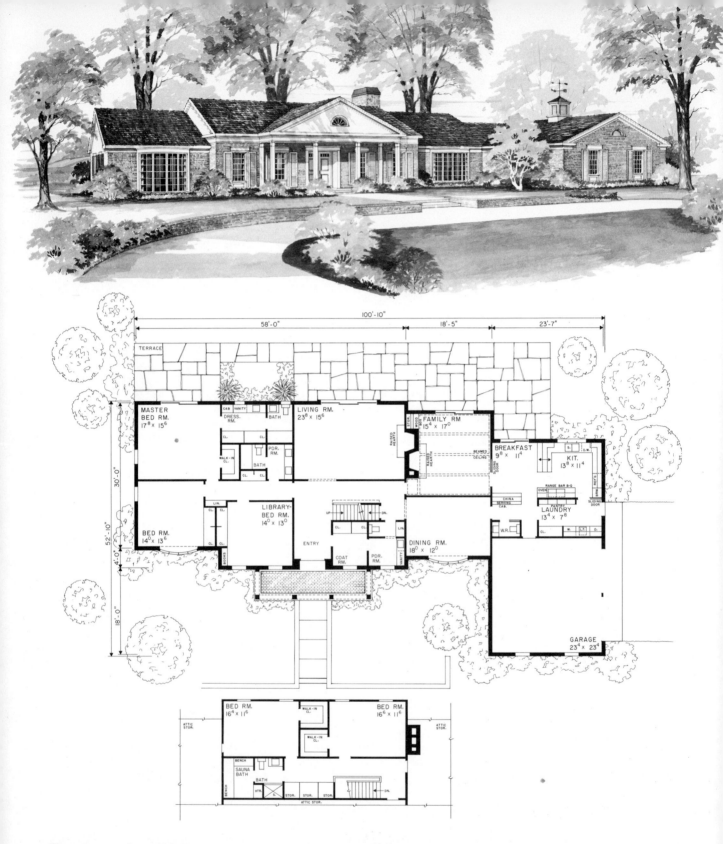

Design S 2133 3,024 Sq. Ft. — First Floor/826 Sq. Ft. — Second Floor/54,883 Cu. Ft.

A country-estate home which will command all the attention it truly deserves. The projecting pediment gable supported by the finely proportioned columns lends an aura of elegance. The window treatment, the front door detailing, the massive, capped, chimney, the cupola, the brick veneer exterior, and the varying roof planes complete the characterization of an impressive home. Inside, there are 3,024 square feet on the first floor. In addition, there is a two bedroom second floor should its development be necessary. However, whether called upon to function as one, or 1-½ story home it will provide a lifetime of gracious living. Don't overlook the compartment baths, the big library, the coat room, the beamed ceiling family room, the two fireplaces.

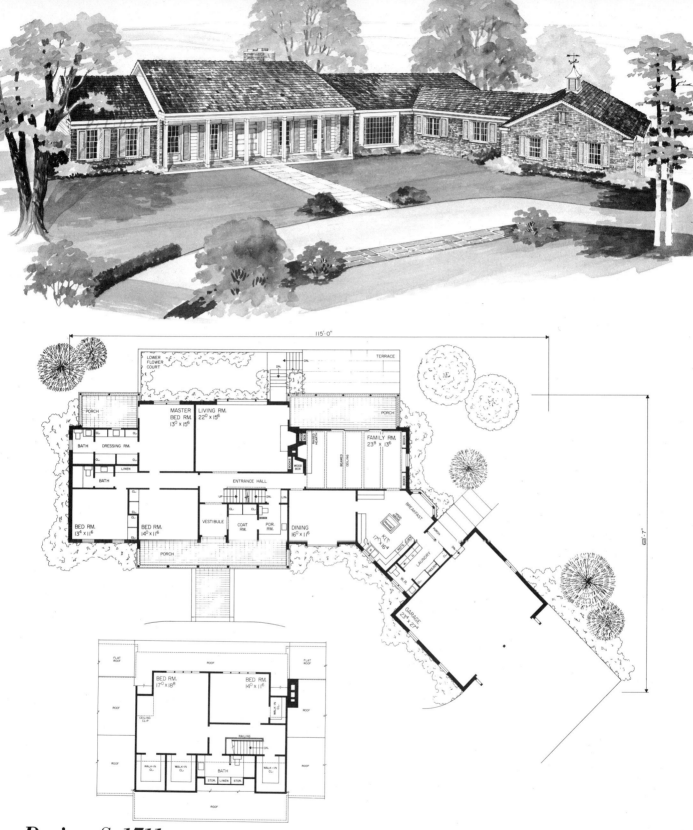

Design S 1711 2,580 Sq. Ft. — First Floor/938 Sq. Ft. — Second Floor/46,788 Cu. Ft.

If the gracious charm of the Colonial South appeals to you, this may be just the house you've been waiting for. There is something solid and dependable in its well-balanced facade and wide, pillared front porch. Much of the interest generated by this design comes from its interesting expanses of roof and angular projection of its kitchen and garage. The feeling of elegance is further experienced upon stepping inside, through double doors, to the spacious entrance hall where there is the separate coat room. Adjacent to this is the powder room, also convenient from the living areas. Work area of kitchen and laundry room is truly outstanding. Designed as a five bedroom house, each is large. Storage and bath facilities are excellent. Truly, an unforgettable family home!

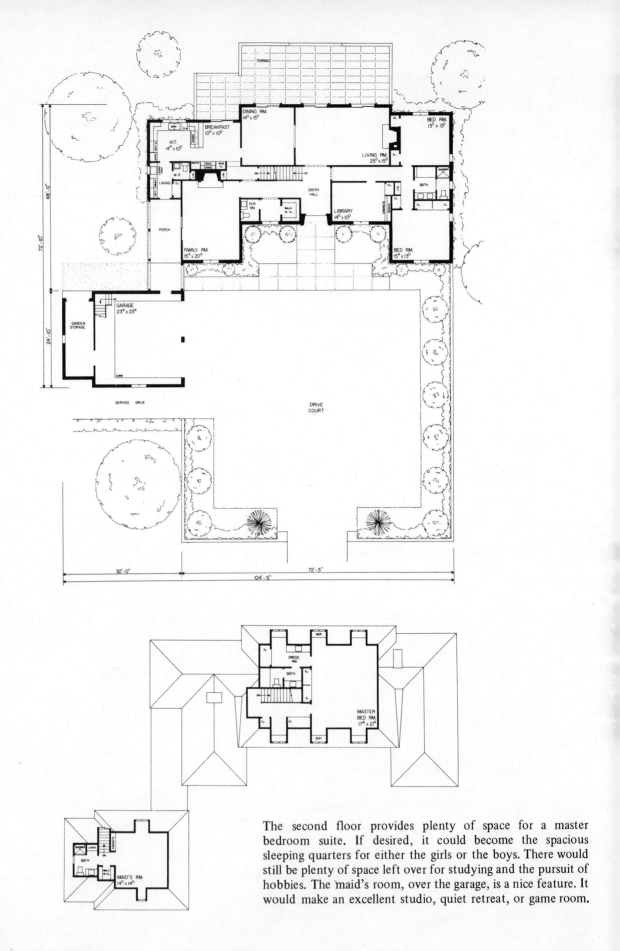

The second floor provides plenty of space for a master bedroom suite. If desired, it could become the spacious sleeping quarters for either the girls or the boys. There would still be plenty of space left over for studying and the pursuit of hobbies. The maid's room, over the garage, is a nice feature. It would make an excellent studio, quiet retreat, or game room.

Design S 1993 2,658 Sq. Ft. — First Floor/840 Sq. Ft. — Master Suite/376 Sq. Ft. — Maid's Suite/57,057 Cu. Ft.

Exquisite Good Taste - French Provincial

The elegance of pleasing proportion and delightful detailing has seldom been better exemplified than by this classic French country manor adaptation. Approaching the house across the drive court, the majesty of this multi-roofed structure is breathtaking, indeed. While there is an aura of old world formality, there is also an accompanying feeling of contemporary livability. The graciousness with which it will unfold, will be awaiting only the arrival of the occupants; for all the elements are present to guarantee complete livability both indoors and out. A trip through the house reveals a fine arrangement of large rooms. If necessary, the library may be called upon to become the fourth bedroom. Observe the work center. Don't miss garden storage room and covered porch.

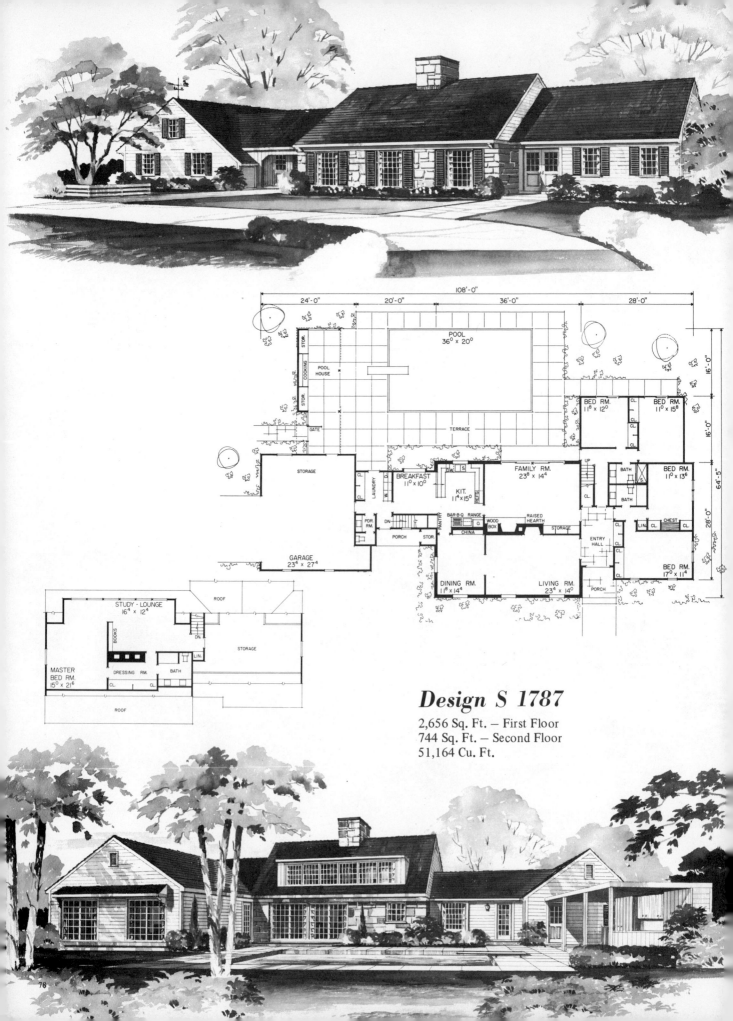

108'-0"

24'-0" 20'-0" 36'-0" 28'-0"

16'-0"

16'-0"

64'-5"

28'-0"

POOL
36⁰ x 20⁰

STOR.
COOKING
POOL HOUSE
STOR.
GATE

TERRACE

BED RM.
11⁸ x 12⁰
CL.

BED RM.
11⁰ x 15⁶
CL.
CL.

STORAGE

CL.
LAUNDRY
W.
CL.

BREAKFAST
11⁰ x 10⁰

KIT.
11⁴ x 15⁰

D.W.
S.

FAMILY RM.
23⁸ x 14⁴

UP
CL.

BATH
BATH
S.

BED RM.
11⁰ x 13⁶

PDR. RM.
DN.
PORCH
STOR.
PANTRY

BAR-B-Q RANGE
WOOD BOX
CHINA

RAISED HEARTH
STORAGE

ENTRY HALL

LIN. CL.
CHEST
CL.

GARAGE
23⁴ x 27⁴

DINING RM.
11⁸ x 14⁴

LIVING RM.
23⁴ x 14⁰

PORCH

BED RM.
17⁰ x 11⁴

STUDY - LOUNGE
16⁴ x 12⁴

ROOF

ROOF

STORAGE

BOOKS
DN.

LIN.

MASTER
BED RM.
15⁰ x 21⁶

DRESSING RM.
CL. CL.

BATH

ROOF

Design S 1787

2,656 Sq. Ft. — First Floor
744 Sq. Ft. — Second Floor
51,164 Cu. Ft.

1½-Story Homes

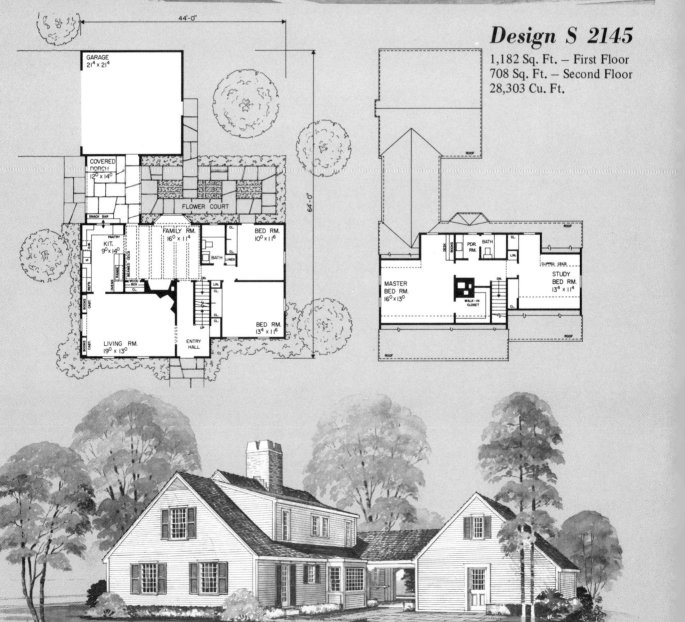

Design S 2145

1,182 Sq. Ft. — First Floor
708 Sq. Ft. — Second Floor
28,303 Cu. Ft.

44'-0"

64'-0"

GARAGE
21⁴ x 21⁴

COVERED PORCH
12⁰ x 14⁰

FLOWER COURT

SNACK BAR

PANTRY

KIT.
9⁰ x 14⁰

WOOD BOX

BEAMED CEILING

FAMILY RM.
16⁰ x 11⁴

BATH

LINEN

CL.

BED RM.
10⁰ x 11⁶

LIVING RM.
19⁰ x 13⁰

ENTRY HALL

UP

CL.

BED RM.
13⁴ x 11⁶

ROOF

MASTER BED RM.
16⁰ x 13⁰

WALK-IN CLOSET

DN.

DESK

BOOKS

PDR. RM.

BATH

LIN.

CLIPPED CEIL.

STUDY BED RM.
13⁴ x 11⁴

ROOF

ROOF

Design S 1701

1,344 Sq. Ft. — First Floor
948 Sq. Ft. — Second Floor
33,952 Cu. Ft.

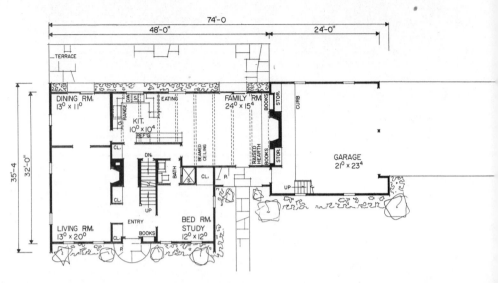

Design S 1736

1,618 Sq. Ft. — First Floor
952 Sq. Ft. — Second Floor
34,106 Cu. Ft.

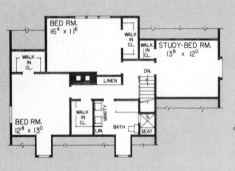

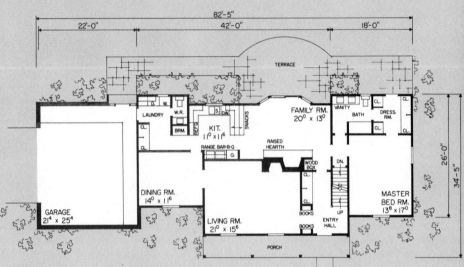

Design S 1793

1,986 Sq. Ft. — First Floor
944 Sq. Ft. — Second Floor
35,800 Cu. Ft.

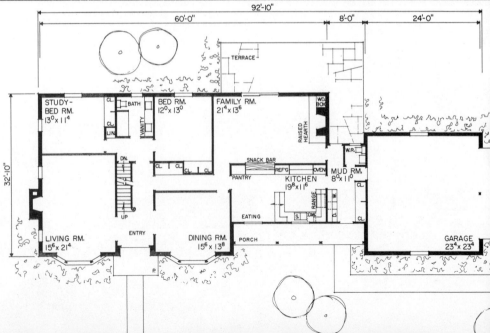

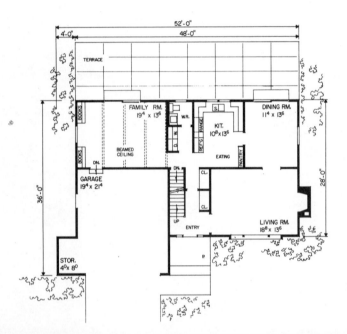

Design S 1241

1,064 Sq. Ft. – First Floor
898 Sq. Ft. – Second Floor
24,723 Cu. Ft.

You don't need a mansion to live graciously. What you do need is a practical floor plan which takes into consideration the varied activities of the busy family. This story-and-a-half design will not require a large piece of property. Its living potential is tremendous.

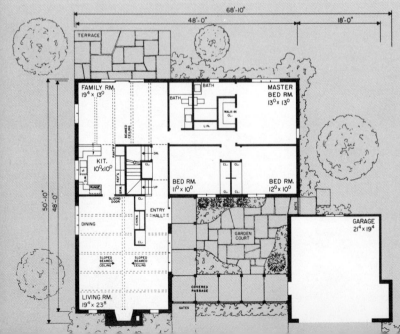

Design S 2127

1,712 Sq. Ft. – First Floor
450 Sq. Ft. – Second Floor
39,435 Cu. Ft.

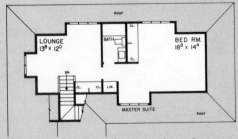

Features aplenty — both inside and out. A list of the exterior design highlights is most interesting. It begins with the character created by the impressive roof surfaces. The U-shape creates a unique appeal and results in the formation of a garden court.

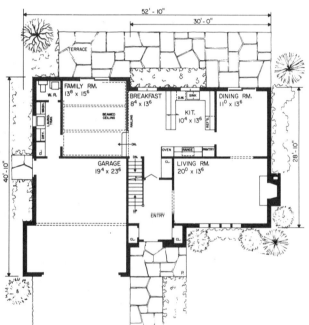

Design S 1991

1,262 Sq. Ft. — First Floor
1,108 Sq. Ft. — Second Floor
20,270 Cu. Ft.

Put yourself and your family in this English cottage adaptation and you'll all rejoice over your new home for many a year. The pride of owning and living in a home that is distinctive will be a constant source of satisfaction. Count the features that will serve your family for years.

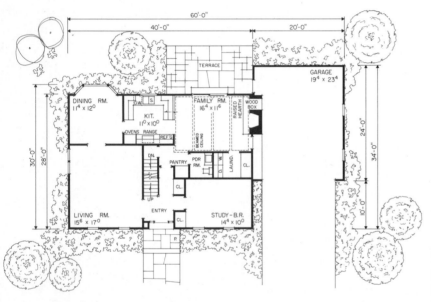

Design S 1791

1,157 Sq. Ft. — First Floor
875 Sq. Ft. — Second Floor
27,790 Cu. Ft.

Wherever you build this little house an aura of Cape Cod is sure to unfold. The symmetry is pleasing, indeed. The authentic center entrance projects a beckoning call.

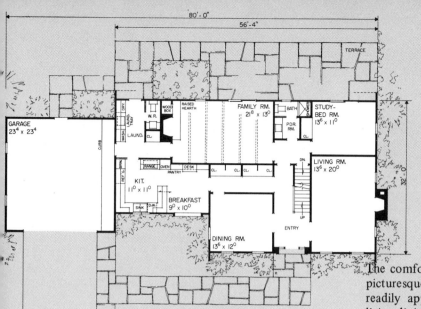

Design S 1987

1,632 Sq. Ft. — First Floor
912 Sq. Ft. — Second Floor
35,712 Cu. Ft.

The comforts of home will be endless when enjoyed in this picturesque Colonial adaptation. And the reasons why are readily apparent. Note cozy family room, study, formal living dining room, etc.

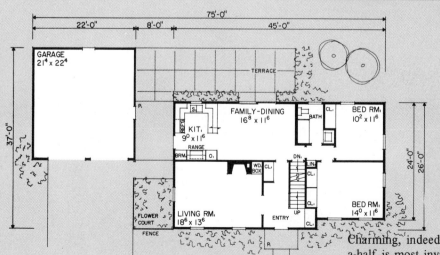

Design S 3126

1,141 Sq. Ft. — First Floor
630 Sq. Ft. — Second Floor
25,533 Cu. Ft.

Charming, indeed! The traditional flavor of this story-and-a-half is most inviting. As an expandable house this design will be hard to beat. There is a full basement for extra recreational space.

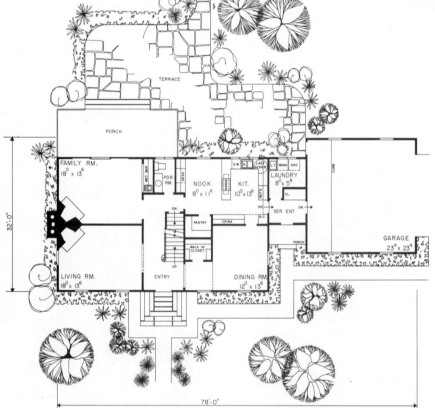

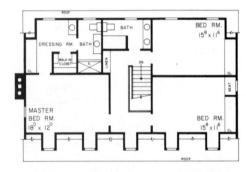

Design S 2520

1,419 Sq. Ft. — First Floor
1,040 Sq. Ft. — Second Floor
39,370 Cu. Ft.

From Tidewater Virginia comes this historic adaptation, a positive reminder of the charm of Early American architecture. Note how the center entrance gives birth to fine traffic circulation. List the numerous features.

Design S 1970

1,664 Sq. Ft.—First Floor
1,116 Sq. Ft.—Second Floor
41,912 Cu. Ft.

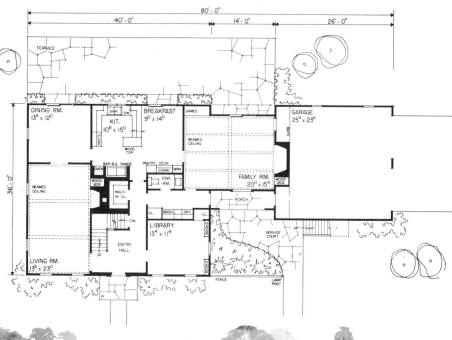

The prototype of this colonial house was an integral part of the 18th-Century New England landscape; the updated version is a welcome addition to any suburban scene. Main entry wing, patterned after classic Cape Cod cottage design, is two stories high but has a pleasing groundhugging look. Steeply pitched roof, triple dormers, and massive central chimney anchor the house firmly to its site. Entry elevation is symmetrically balanced; doorway, middle dormer, and chimney are in perfect alignment. One-story wide—windowed wing is a spacious beam-ceilinged family room with splay-walled entry porch on front elevation, sliding glass windows at the rear, opening to terrace.

Design S 1242 1,872 Sq. Ft.-First Floor

982 Sq. Ft.-Second Floor 29,221 Cu. Ft.

Here are three long, low one-and-a-half story designs with all the traditional charm one would wish for his new home. The floor plans offer all the livability an active family would want. Which is your favorite design?

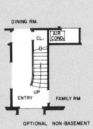

OPTIONAL NON-BASEMENT

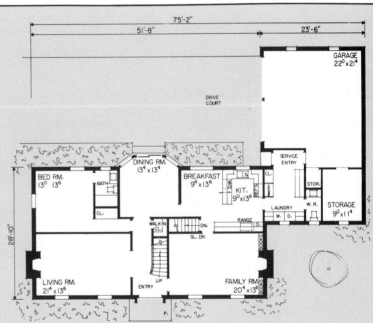

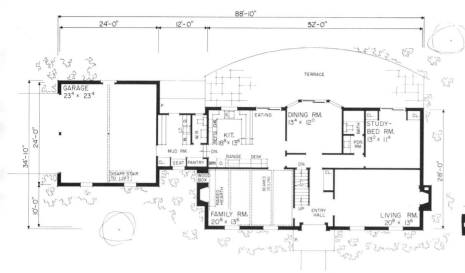

Design S 1747

1,690 Sq. Ft.-First Floor

1,060 Sq. Ft.-Second Floor

38,424 Cu. Ft.

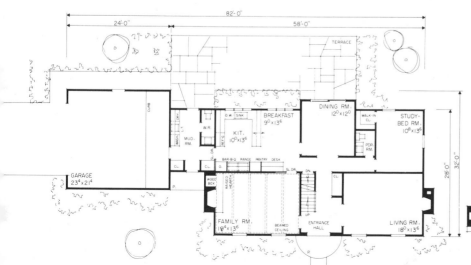

Design S 1906

1,514 Sq. Ft.-First Floor

992 Sq. Ft.-Second Floor

37,311 Cu. Ft.

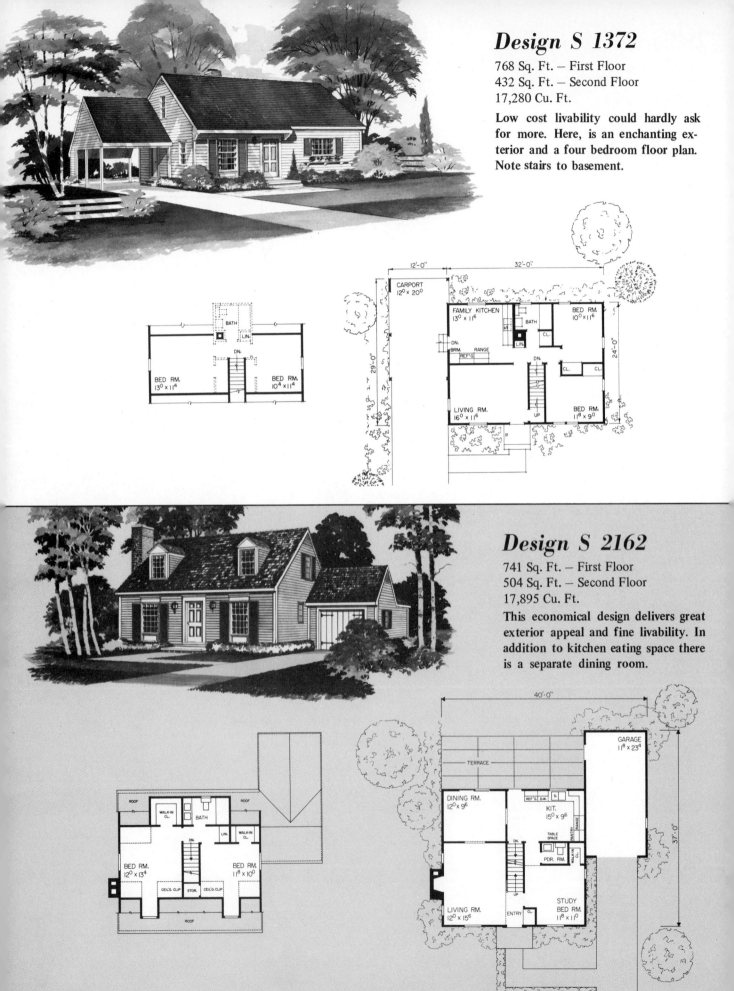

Design S 1372

768 Sq. Ft. — First Floor
432 Sq. Ft. — Second Floor
17,280 Cu. Ft.

Low cost livability could hardly ask for more. Here, is an enchanting exterior and a four bedroom floor plan. Note stairs to basement.

BATH
LIN.
DN.
BED RM. 13⁰ x 11⁴
BED RM. 10⁴ x 11⁴

12'-0"   32'-0"

CARPORT 12⁰ x 20⁰

FAMILY KITCHEN 13⁰ x 11⁶
BATH
CL.
BED RM. 10⁰ x 11⁶
DN.
BRM.   RANGE
REF'G
LIN.
CL.
CL.
29'-0"   24'-0"
DN.
UP
LIVING RM. 16⁰ x 11⁶
BED RM. 11⁸ x 9⁰

Design S 2162

741 Sq. Ft. — First Floor
504 Sq. Ft. — Second Floor
17,895 Cu. Ft.

This economical design delivers great exterior appeal and fine livability. In addition to kitchen eating space there is a separate dining room.

ROOF
WALK-IN CL.
BATH
ROOF
WALK-IN CL.
LIN.
DN.
BED RM. 12⁰ x 13⁴
BED RM. 11⁸ x 10⁰
CEIL'G. CLIP   STOR.   CEIL'G. CLIP
ROOF

40'-0"

TERRACE
GARAGE 11⁸ x 23⁴
DINING RM. 12⁰ x 9⁶
REF'G D.W.
KIT. 15⁰ x 9⁶
RANGE
PANTRY
TABLE SPACE
DN.
PDR. RM.
WALK-IN CL.
37'-0"
LIVING RM. 12⁰ x 15⁶
ENTRY   CL.
UP
STUDY BED RM. 11⁸ x 11⁰

Design S 1394

832 Sq. Ft. – First Floor
512 Sq. Ft. – Second Floor
18,453 Cu. Ft.

The growing family with a restricted building budget will find this a great investment - a convenient living floor plan inside an attractive facade.

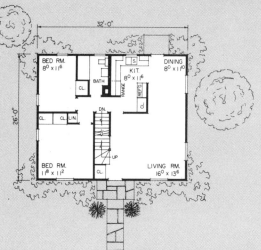

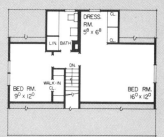

Design S 2510

1,191 Sq. Ft. – First Floor
533 Sq. Ft. – Second Floor
27,500 Cu. Ft.

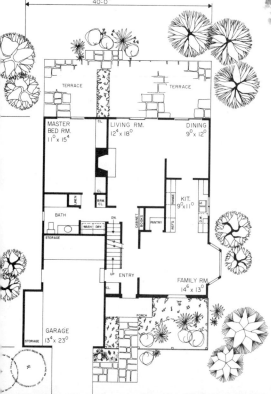

The pleasant in-line kitchen is flanked by a separate dining room and a family room. The master bedroom is on the first floor with two more bedrooms upstairs.

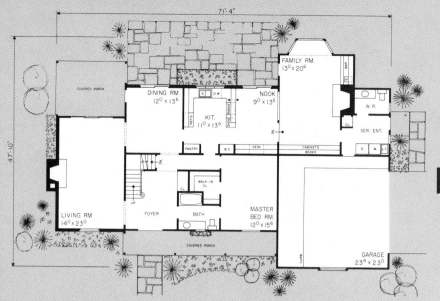

Design S 2500

1,851 Sq. Ft. — First Floor
762 Sq. Ft. — Second Floor
43,052 Cu. Ft.

The large family will enjoy the wonderful living patterns offered by this charming home. Don't miss the covered rear porch, the many features of the family room.

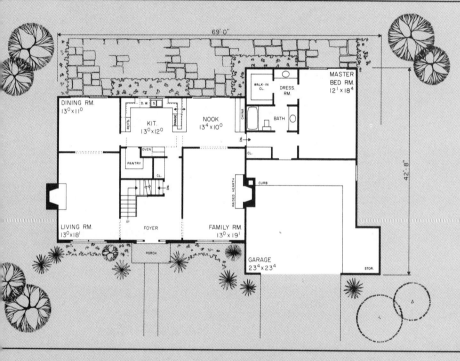

Design S 2501

1,699 Sq. Ft. — First Floor
758 Sq. Ft. — Second Floor
37,693 Cu. Ft.

Whether you build this inviting home with a fieldstone front, or substitute a different material of your choice, you can be assured having selected a great home for your family.

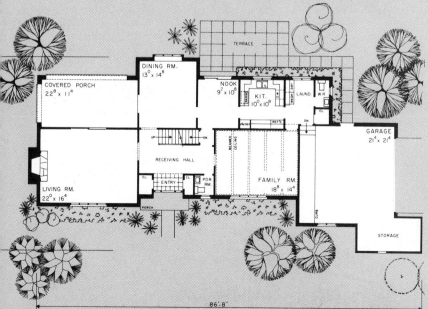

Design S 2338

1,505 Sq. Ft. — First Floor
1,219 Sq. Ft. — Second Floor
38,878 Cu. Ft.

A spacious receiving hall is a fine setting for the welcoming of guests. Here traffic flows effectively to all areas of the plan. Outstanding livability.

Design S 2286

1,496 Sq. Ft. — First Floor
751 Sq. Ft. — Second Floor
32,165 Cu. Ft.

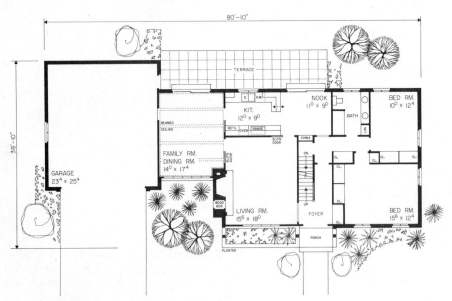

A touch of Tudor styling houses four bedrooms, two baths, and a sizeable family dining room with a cozy beamed ceiling. Note access to rear terrace.

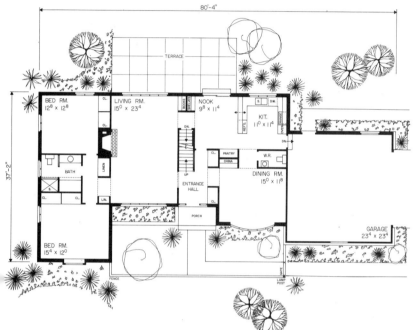

Design S 2284

1,677 Sq. Ft. – First Floor
897 Sq. Ft. – Second Floor
40,413 Cu. Ft.

This low-slung traditional design features four bedrooms plus three baths and a wash room. For family recreational and hobby space there is the basement.

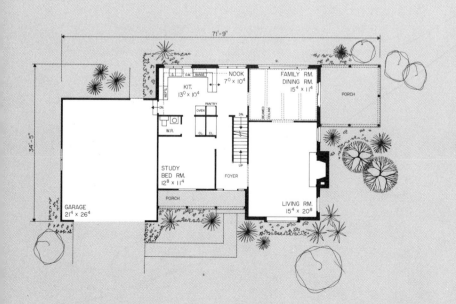

An appealing home for the modest budget. There is exceptional livability for the average sized family. And there is plenty of flexibility. Note room use options.

Design S 2285

1,118 Sq. Ft. – First Floor
821 Sq. Ft. – Second Floor
28,585 Cu. Ft.

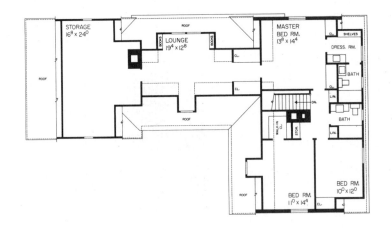

Design S 2174

1,506 Sq. Ft. – First Floor
1,156 Sq. Ft. – Second Floor
37,360 Cu. Ft.

Your building budget could hardly buy more charm, or greater livability. The appeal of the exterior is wrapped up in a myriad of design features. They include: the interesting roof lines; the effective use of brick and horizontal siding; the delightful window treatment; the covered front porch; the chimney and dove-cote detailing. The livability of the interior is represented by a long list of convenient living features. They include: Formal living and dining rooms; informal family room and second floor lounge; extra first floor bedroom with adjacent bath; efficient kitchen and laundry; three bedrooms and two baths upstairs; plenty of closets; bulk storage room over garage. Don't overlook the sliding glass doors, the two fireplaces, the breakfast area, the basement.

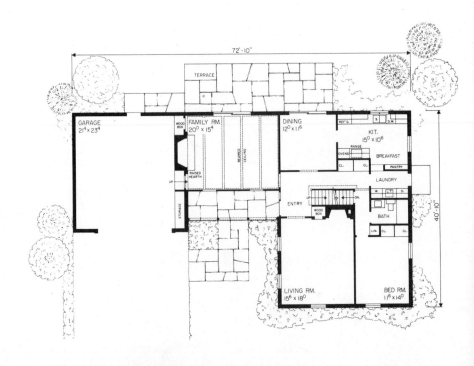

Two-Story Homes

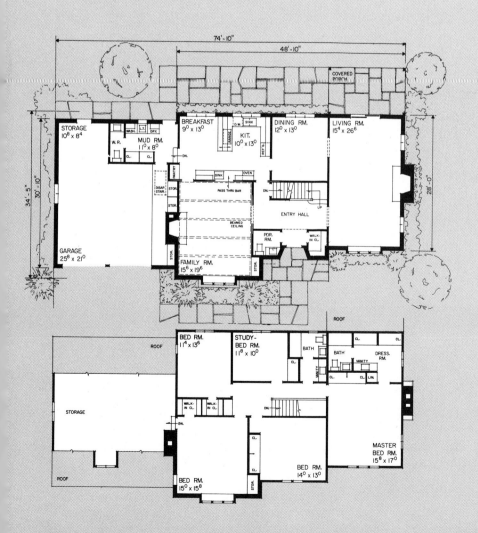

Design S 1988

1,650 Sq. Ft. — First Floor
1,507 Sq. Ft. — Second Floor
49,474 Cu. Ft.

A charming English Tudor adaptation which retains all the appeal of yesteryear, yet features an outstanding and practical contemporary floor plan. With all those rooms to serve a myriad of functions, the active family will lead a glorious existence. Imagine, a five bedroom second floor! Or, make it a four bedroom, plus study, upstairs. In addition to the two full baths and fine closet facilities, there is convenient access to the huge storage area over the garage. Downstairs, flanking the impressive, formal front entry hall, there is space galore. The twenty-six foot, end living room will certainly be a favorite feature. The family room is large and will be lots of fun to furnish. The excellent kitchen is strategically located between the formal dining room and the informal breakfast room. The mud room is ideally located to receive traffic from the garage as well as from the rear yard. Don't miss the wash room and the powder room. Note kitchen/family room pass-thru.

Design S 1887

1,518 Sq. Ft. – First Floor
1,144 Sq. Ft. – Second Floor
40,108 Cu. Ft.

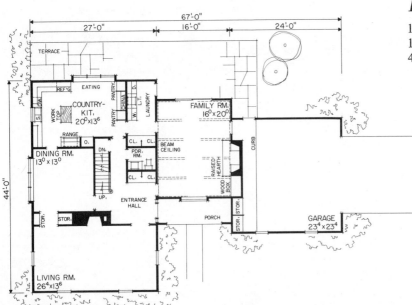

This Gambrel roof Colonial is steeped in history. And well it should be, for its pleasing proportions are a delight to the eye. The various roof planes, the window treatment, and the rambling nature of the entire house revive a picture of rural New England. The covered porch protects the front door which opens into a spacious entrance hall. Traffic then flows in an orderly fashion to the end living room, the separate dining room, the cozy family room, and to the spacious country-kitchen. There is a first floor laundry, plenty of coat closets, and a handy powder room. Two fireplaces enliven the decor of the living areas. Upstairs there is an exceptional master bed-room layout and abundant storage. Note walk-in closets. Garage is over sized and features storage cabinets.

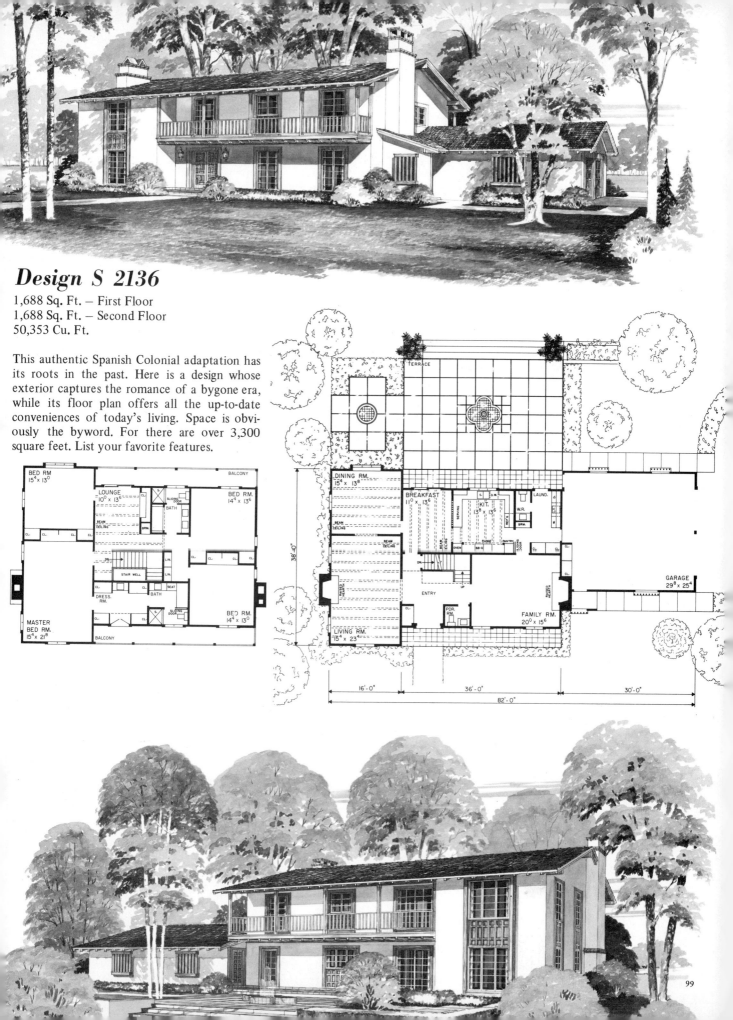

Design S 2136

1,688 Sq. Ft. — First Floor
1,688 Sq. Ft. — Second Floor
50,353 Cu. Ft.

This authentic Spanish Colonial adaptation has its roots in the past. Here is a design whose exterior captures the romance of a bygone era, while its floor plan offers all the up-to-date conveniences of today's living. Space is obviously the byword. For there are over 3,300 square feet. List your favorite features.

The French Mansard roof home is one of the most distinguished of all traditional styles. It has good proportion, delightful symmetry, and a feeling of formality. The recessed center entrance protects the double doors which lead into the entry hall highlighted by the open staircase to the second floor. The traffic patterns of the plan are most flexible and efficient.

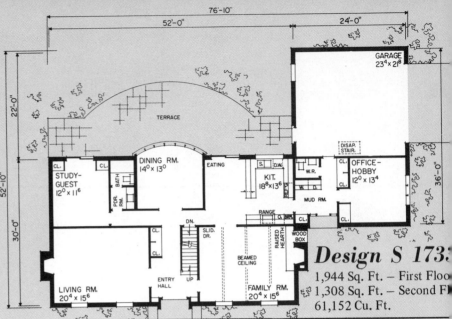

Design S 1733

1,944 Sq. Ft. – First Floor
1,308 Sq. Ft. – Second Floor
61,152 Cu. Ft.

Design S 1951 1,346 Sq. Ft. – First Floor

1,114 Sq. Ft. – Second Floor
39,034 Cu. Ft.

This marvelous French home with its Mansard roof could not be improved upon. Pride of ownership will never diminish for the occupants of this home.

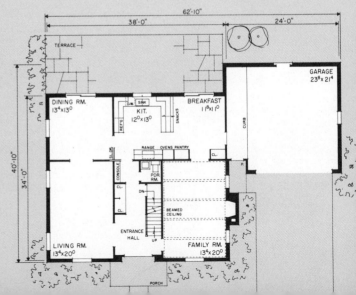

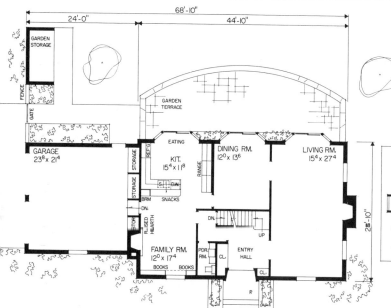

Of French origin, the characteristic feature of this two story design is its Mansard roof. Also, enhancing the formality of its exterior are the beautifully proportioned windows, the recessed front entrance with double doors, the two stately chimneys, and the attached garage.

Design S 1275

1,314 Sq. Ft. — First Floor
1,080 Sq. Ft. — Second Floor
33,656 Cu. Ft.

Design S 2131

1,214 Sq. Ft. – First Floor
1,097 Sq. Ft. – Second Floor
28,070 Cu. Ft.

A Gambrel roof design from our Colonial past. The growing family will have plenty of space in this modest house.

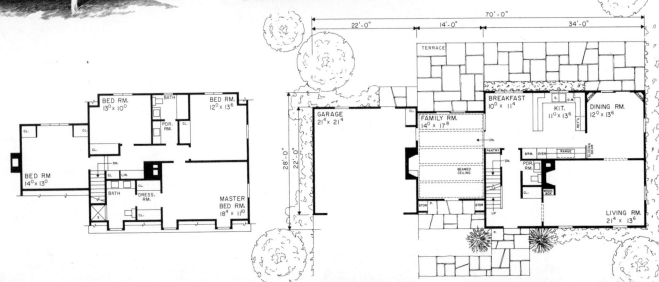

Design S 2189

1,134 Sq. Ft. – First Floor
1,063 Sq. Ft. – Second Floor
31,734 Cu. Ft.

Imagine this Colonial adaptation on your new building site! The symmetry and the pleasing proportion make it a wonderful addition to the local scene.

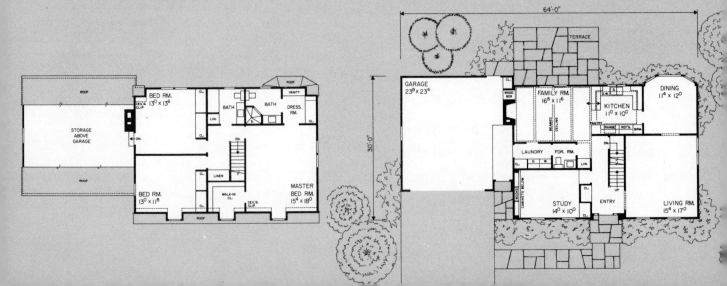

Design S 1827

1,442 Sq. Ft. – First Floor
1,098 Sq. Ft. – Second Floor
35,275 Cu. Ft.

An early Colonial Gambrel-roofed exterior to stir memories of the 18th Century in America. The large family will take pride in this house.

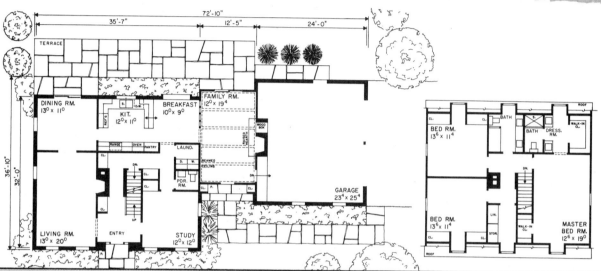

Design S 1777

1,136 Sq. Ft. – First Floor
1,004 Sq. Ft. – Second Floor
32,318 Cu. Ft.

A compact Gambrel with all the features and livability of a much larger home. There are features galore. Don't miss a one!

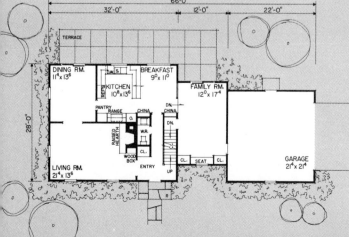

Design S 2276

1,273 Sq. Ft. – First Floor
1,323 Sq. Ft. – Second Floor
40,450 Cu. Ft.

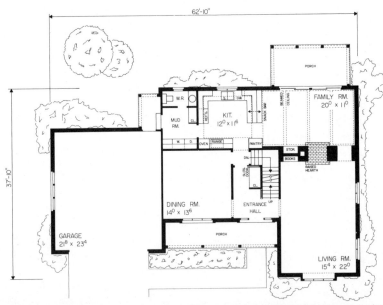

Design S 2274

1,941 Sq. Ft. – First Floor
1,392 Sq. Ft. – Second Floor
32,580 Cu. Ft.

Design S 2324

1,256 Sq. Ft. – First Floor
1,351 Sq. Ft. – Second Floor
37,603 Cu. Ft.

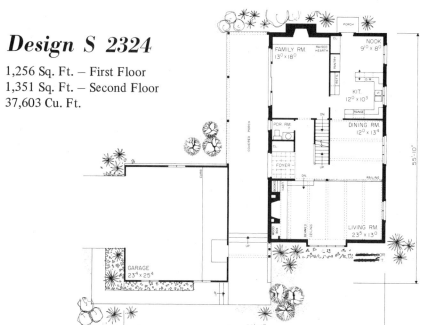

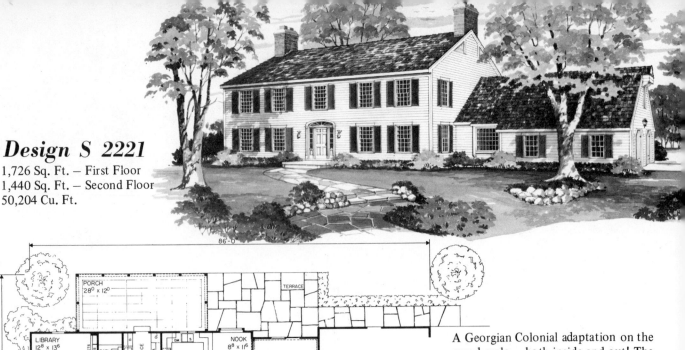

Design S 2221

1,726 Sq. Ft. – First Floor
1,440 Sq. Ft. – Second Floor
50,204 Cu. Ft.

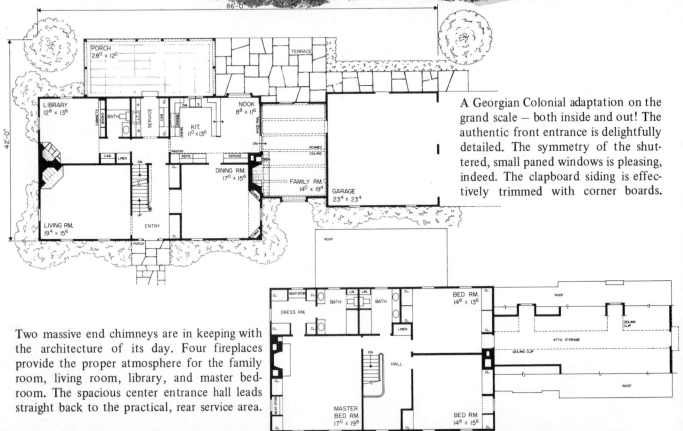

A Georgian Colonial adaptation on the grand scale – both inside and out! The authentic front entrance is delightfully detailed. The symmetry of the shuttered, small paned windows is pleasing, indeed. The clapboard siding is effectively trimmed with corner boards.

Two massive end chimneys are in keeping with the architecture of its day. Four fireplaces provide the proper atmosphere for the family room, living room, library, and master bedroom. The spacious center entrance hall leads straight back to the practical, rear service area.

Design S 1868

1,190 Sq. Ft. – First Floor
1,300 Sq. Ft. – Second Floor
32,327 Cu. Ft.

Design S 2211

1,214 Sq. Ft. — First Floor
1,146 Sq. Ft. — Second Floor
32,752 Cu. Ft.

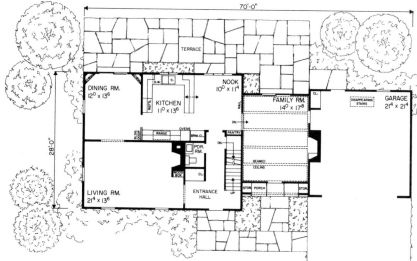

The appeal of this Colonial home will be virtually everlasting. It will improve with age and service the growing family well. The architectural detailing is exquisite, indeed. The window treatment, the narrow siding, the massive chimneys, the service porch and the garage are attractive features.

Imagine your family living here. There are four bedrooms, 2½ baths, a formal and an informal living area, two fireplaces, a separate dining room, a breakfast nook, an efficient work center, and a basement. Sliding glass doors lead from dining and family rooms to rear terraces.

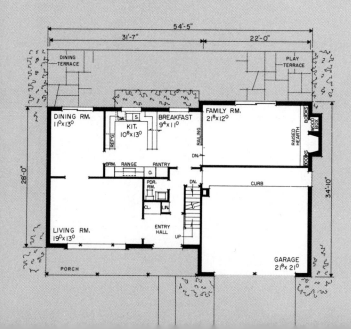

For the large family — a second floor featuring five bedrooms, three full baths, and plenty of closet space! Downstairs, there are two big living areas, two sizeable dining areas, two sets of sliding glass doors, an outstanding kitchen and handy powder room. Note fireplace.

Design S 1767

1,510 Sq. Ft. – First Floor
1,406 Sq. Ft. – Second Floor
42,070 Cu. Ft.

An impressive Georgian adaptation that even at first glance seems to have a story of livability to tell. From the spacious center entry hall traffic can flow conveniently to all areas. And what delightful areas they are!

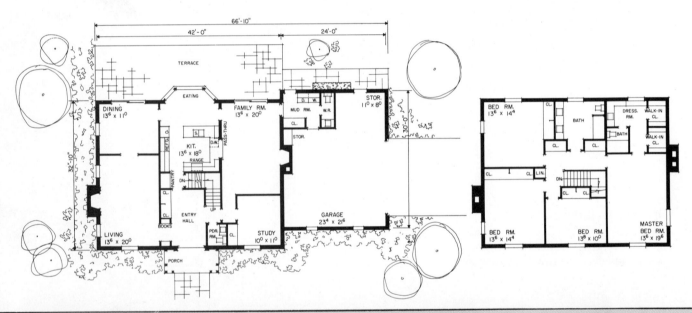

You'll never regret your choice of this Georgian design. Its stately facade seems to foretell all of the exceptional features to be found inside. From the delightfully spacious front entry hall, to the studio or maid's room over the garage this home is unique all along the way.

Design S 1858

1,794 Sq. Ft. – First Floor
1,474 Sq. Ft. – Second Floor
424 Sq. Ft. – Studio/54,878 Cu. Ft.

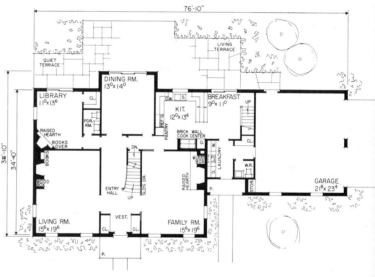

Design S 1774

1,574 Sq. Ft. – First Floor
1,124 Sq. Ft. – Second Floor
37,616 Cu. Ft.

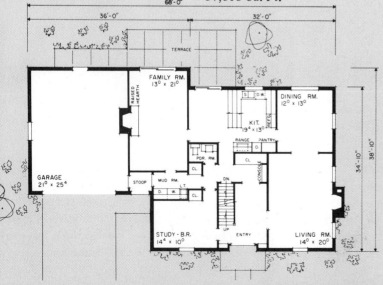

Reminiscent of 18-Century homes of French provinces, this country house has a brick exterior with a Mansard roof and repeated, soft-curved arches over windows and doors. Inside, the house is well arranged for today's living requirements.

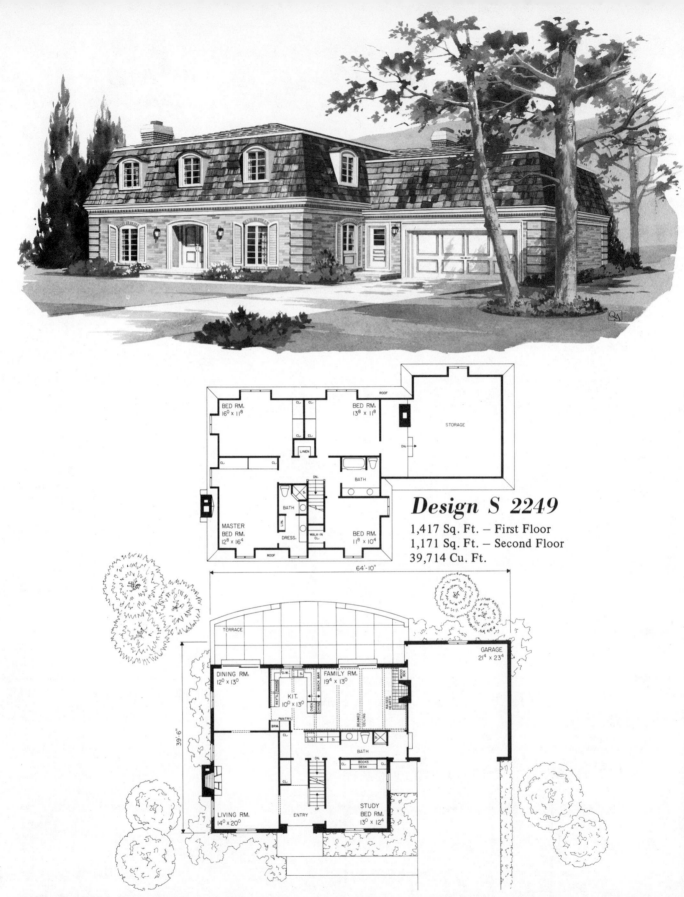

Design S 2249

1,417 Sq. Ft. — First Floor
1,171 Sq. Ft. — Second Floor
39,714 Cu. Ft.

The formality of French design is certainly impressive. This Mansard version has a noticeably hipped roof. The delicate nature of the exterior's architectural detailing is pleasing to behold. The double front doors are recessed and open to a center entrance hall. The interior layout is practical and, indeed, efficient. The end living and dining rooms will foster formal living patterns, while the outstanding kitchen and family room will function together in a delightfully informal fashion. Further, there is the quiet study. Upstairs, there are four excellent bedrooms, and two full baths.

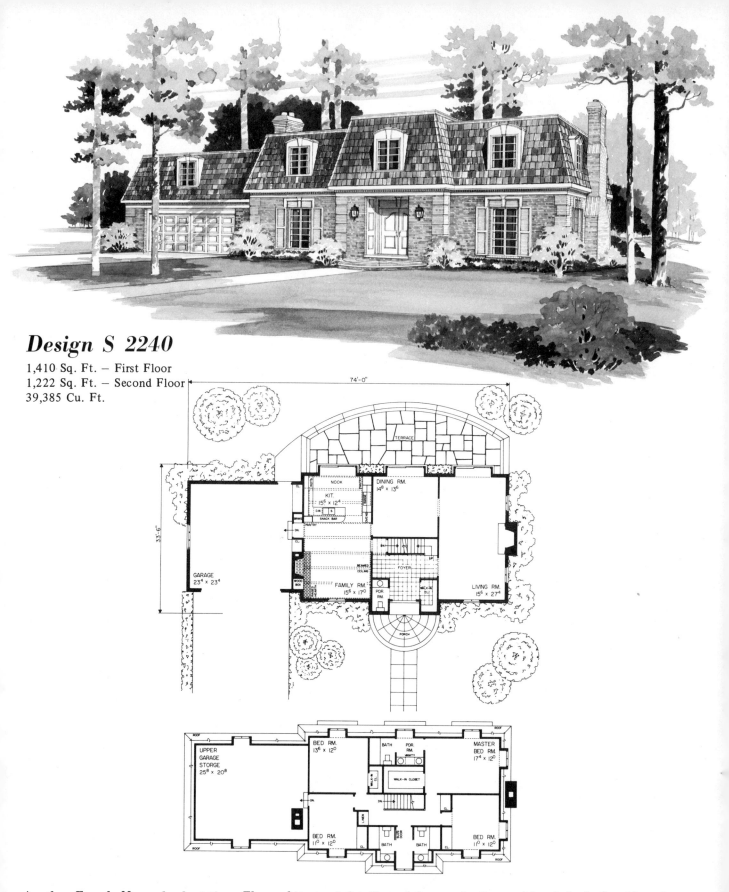

Design S 2240

1,410 Sq. Ft. – First Floor
1,222 Sq. Ft. – Second Floor
39,385 Cu. Ft.

Another French Mansard adaptation. The architectural detailing of its exterior is exquisite, indeed. Consider: the pleasing proportions; the window, door and chimney treatment; the brick quoins at the corners; the carriage lamps and dentils at the cornice line. Inside, there is the formal foyer, plus the formal and the informal living areas. Upstairs there are four bedrooms and three full baths. Don't overlook the sliding glass doors to the rear terrace, the two fireplaces, the extra powder room, the beamed ceiling, and the generous storage facility over the garage.

Design S 2128

1,152 Sq. Ft. — First Floor
896 Sq. Ft. — Second Floor/30,707 Cu. Ft.

Here is proof that your restricted building budget can return to you wonderfully pleasing design and loads of livability. This is an English Tudor adaptation that will surely become your subdivision's favorite facade. Its mark of individuality is obvious to all.

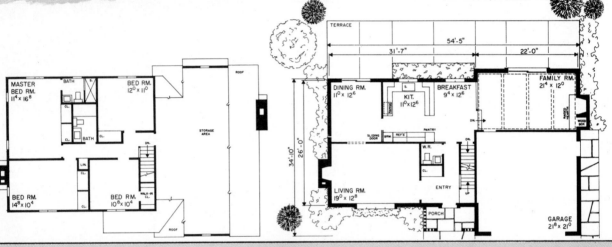

Design S 1856

1,023 Sq. Ft. — First Floor
784 Sq. Ft. — Second Floor/25,570 Cu. Ft.

Small house with big house features and livability. Some of the features are two full baths and extra storage upstairs; laundry, wash room, two fireplaces, downstairs. The pantry is above the wood box and accessible from the kitchen which has eating space.

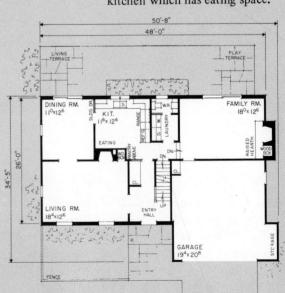

This is a Gambrel roof design. Its distinctive appearance spells charm wherever it may be situated — far out in the country, or on a busy thoroughfare. Compact and economical to build, it will be easy on the budget. In spite of its cost-saving size it is long on livability. It even has a big family room on the second floor!

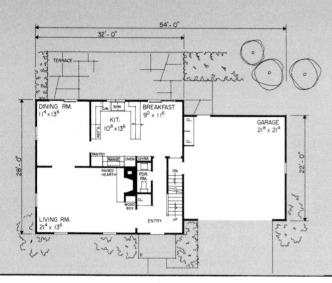

Design S 1986

896 Sq. Ft. — First Floor
1,148 Sq. Ft. — Second Floor/28,840 Cu. Ft.

Truly a picture house. This attractive home with its authentic detailing illustrates how good, good floor planning really can be. All the elements are present for efficient and comfortable living. Try to envision how your family will function here.

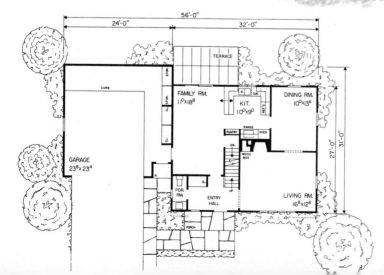

Design S 1719

864 Sq. Ft. — First Floor
896 Sq. Ft. — Second Floor/26,024 Cu. Ft.

113

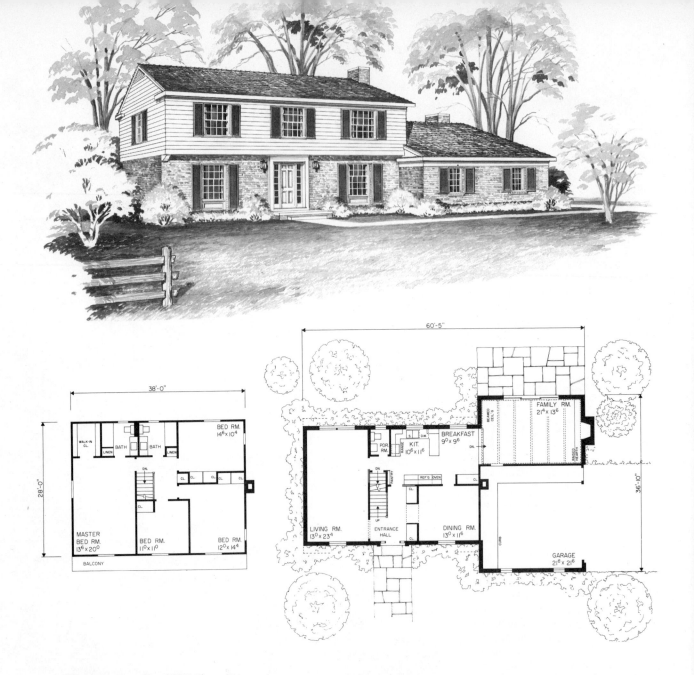

Design S 1715   1,276 Sq. Ft. — First Floor/1,064 Sq. Ft. — Second Floor/31,295 Cu. Ft.

The blueprints you order for this design show details for building each of these three appealing exteriors. Which do you like best? Whatever your choice, the interior will provide the growing family with all the facilities for fine living.

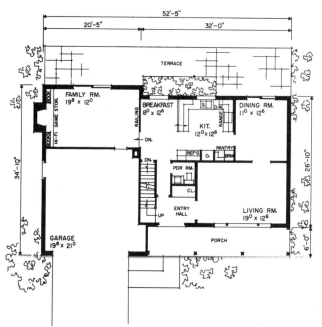

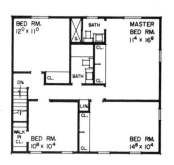

OPTIONAL   NON-BASEMENT

Design S 1333

1,122 Sq. Ft. — First Floor/896 Sq. Ft. — Second Floor
28,141 Cu. Ft.

Here is a great, basic two story plan which offers loads of livability. The construction blueprints come with a number of options. You'll be able to build any of these three exteriors with or without a basement.

Design S 2295

1,947 Sq. Ft. – First Floor
1,092 Sq. Ft. – Second Floor
43,795 Cu. Ft.

This L-shaped two-story will make efficient use of your building site. The floor plan and how it functions is extremely interesting and practical. Study it carefully.

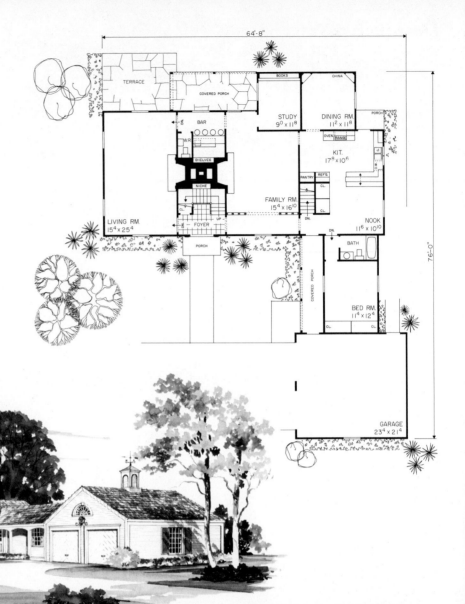

Angular in its configuration, this inviting home offers loads of livability. There are four bedrooms, study, family room, and a 27 foot long living room!

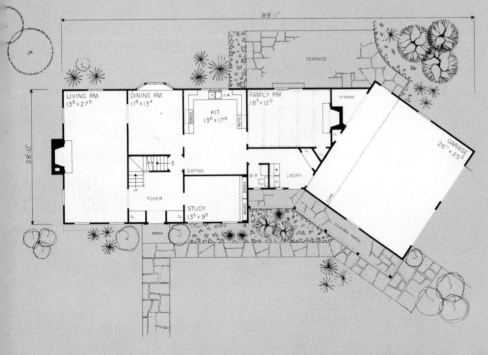

Design S 2322

1,480 Sq. Ft. – First Floor
1,172 Sq. Ft. – Second Floor
41,112 Cu. Ft.

Design S 2346

1,510 Sq. Ft. — First Floor
1,009 Sq. Ft. — Second Floor
36,482 Cu. Ft.

A fine mixture of exterior materials, window treatment, and roof planes help set the character here. Envision your family enjoying all that this design has to offer.

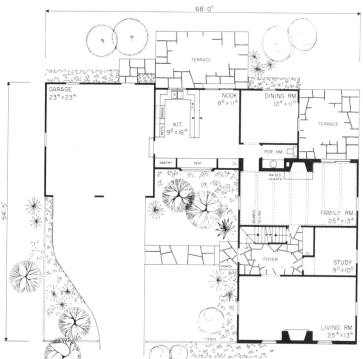

Design S 1269

1,232 Sq. Ft. — First Floor
1,232 Sq. Ft. — Second Floor
33,344 Cu. Ft.

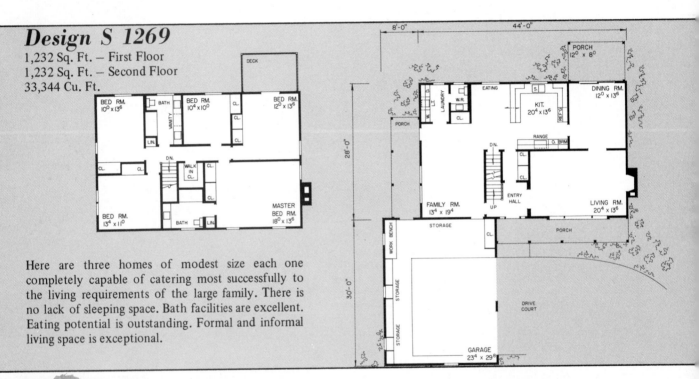

Here are three homes of modest size each one completely capable of catering most successfully to the living requirements of the large family. There is no lack of sleeping space. Bath facilities are excellent. Eating potential is outstanding. Formal and informal living space is exceptional.

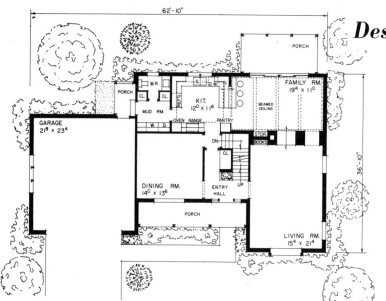

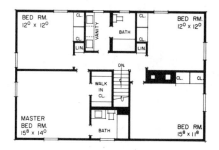

Design S 1082

1,254 Sq. Ft. — First Floor
1,096 Sq. Ft. — Second Floor
37,239 Cu. Ft.

Picking the outstanding feature of this design would certainly be difficult. It has many. Which are your family's favorite highlights?

Design S 1972

1,286 Sq. Ft. — First Floor
960 Sq. Ft. — Second Floor
30,739 Cu. Ft.

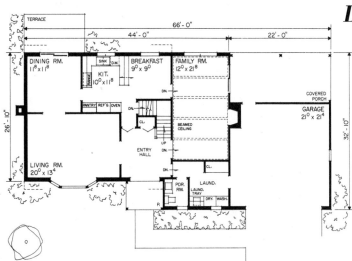

What an appealingly different type of two-story home! It's one whose grace and charm project an aura of welcome. A covered porch protects the double front doors.

Design S 1208

1,170 Sq. Ft. — First Floor/768 Sq. Ft. — Second Floor/26,451 Cu. Ft.

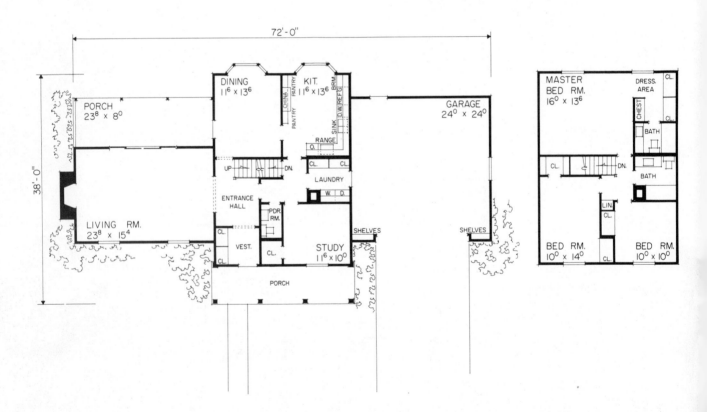

Reminiscent of the stately grandeur of Mount Vernon, this two-story with its living room and garage wings, is yet another example of an earlier era recaptured. Up-to-date floor planning retains a feeling of gracious formality in a most convenient and efficient manner. A highlight of the plan is the living room. Entirely removed from the traffic patterns, it will surely enjoy its full measure of privacy. The separate dining room is ideally situated to be easily serviced from the kitchen, and able to look out upon the rear yard. The covered porch will be a favorite spot for summer relaxation. Then there is the private study, the first floor laundry.

Design S 1816

2,036 Sq. Ft. – First Floor/1,836 Sq. Ft. – Second Floor/55,566 Cu. Ft.

The influence of the Colonial South is delightfully apparent in this gracious two-story design. The stately columns of the front porch set the stage for a memorable visit. The entry hall is impressive with its open stairway. The coat room and powder room are just around the corner. The large, country kitchen will be sheer delight in which to work and, yes, even congregate. There are two big living areas, a separate dining room and a study. Note the front service entrance and the access to the rear yard. Upstairs there are five bedrooms, three baths and plenty of closets. Don't miss the sweeping balcony which overlooks the rear yard or the garage layout with all that storage.

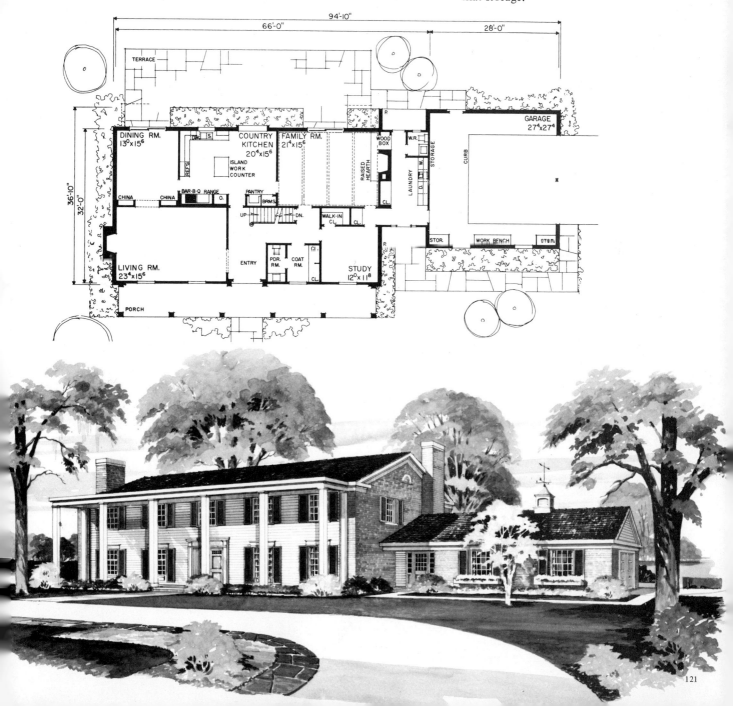

Design S 1285

1,210 Sq. Ft. — First Floor
896 Sq. Ft. — Second Floor
27,385 Cu. Ft.

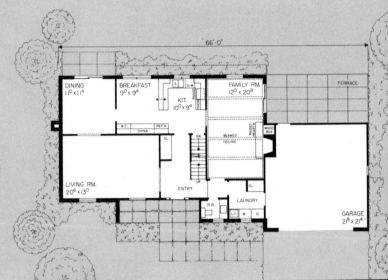

Designed for years of livability. And what great livability this two-story traditional has to offer. The spacious center entry hall routes traffic conveniently to all areas. The formal living room is big and features two windows overlooking the front yard. The separate dining room is but a step from its own terrace. A convenient spot to enjoy dessert, or a second cup of coffee. The breakfast room, the kitchen, and the family room all look out upon the rear yard. A china storage wall will be a popular feature.

Design S 1996

1,056 Sq. Ft. — First Floor
1,040 Sq. Ft. — Second Floor
29,071 Cu. Ft.

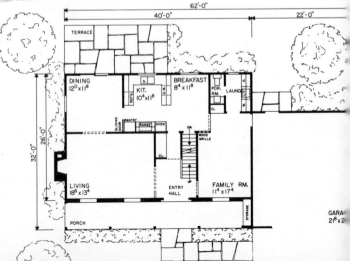

Here is a Farmhouse adaptation with a delightful mixture of natural stone and narrow, horizontal siding. The covered front porch extends across the entire front affording protection for the large windows and the double front doors. The center entry hall dispatches traffic most effectively. The room relationships are outstanding. The fine work center is strategically located between the formal dining and informal breakfast rooms. While there is a basement, there is also a separate first floor laundry with adjacent wash room. Upstairs, four bedrooms, two full baths with twin lavatories and plenty of closets.

Design S 1181

1,186 Sq. Ft. — First Floor
896 Sq. Ft. — Second Floor
28,324 Cu. Ft.

The exterior of this friendly and inviting house is highlighted by the long and low porch which extends the full width of the facade. The inside is cleverly planned to result in two main first floor zones. The formal living zone is comprised of the dining and living rooms which can be free of unnecessary traffic. The informal zone stretches more than 40 feet across the rear and features the U-shaped kitchen, the breakfast room, and the sunken family room. Four bedrooms and two baths make up the second floor.

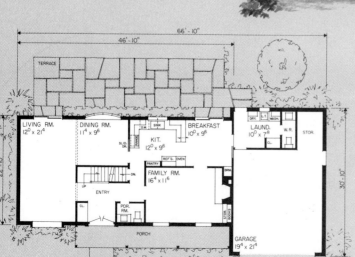

Design S 1933

1,184 Sq. Ft. — First Floor
884 Sq. Ft. — Second Floor
27,976 Cu. Ft.

Picturesque and practical too. As you step into the large, formal front entry you are immediately aware of the efficient and orderly traffic patterns. The first glimpse you get of the end living room will bring to mind the thought of spaciousness. As you turn to the right, past the powder room, you'll notice the front family room. A preferred location for those who don't want their family room to function with the outdoor living areas. Then, of course, there's the fine four bedroom, two bath upstairs.

Design S 2525

919 Sq. Ft. — First Floor
949 Sq. Ft. — Second Floor
29,200 Cu. Ft.

Here is an economically built home that can be constructed with either of the two illustrated exteriors. Which is your favorite? The two study areas provide plenty of multi-purpose, informal living space.

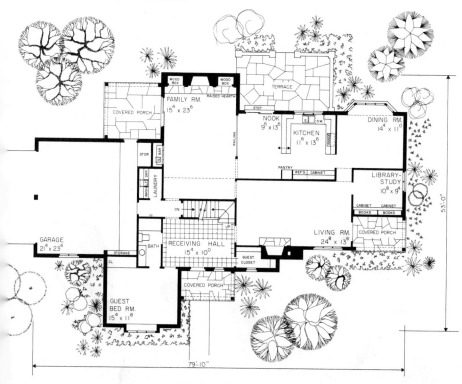

Design S 2356

1,969 Sq. Ft. — First Floor
1,702 Sq. Ft. — Second Floor
55,105 Cu. Ft.

Here is truly an exquisite Tudor adaptation. The exterior, with its interesting roof lines, its window treatment, its stately chimney, and its appealing use of brick and stucco, could hardly be more dramatic. Inside, the drama really begins to unfold as one envisions his family's living patterns. The delightfully large receiving hall has a two story ceiling and controls the flexible traffic patterns. The living and dining rooms, with the library nearby, will cater to the formal living pursuits. The guest room offers another haven for the enjoyment of peace and quiet. Observe the adjacent full bath. Just inside the entrance from the garage is the laundry room. For the family's informal living activities there are the inter-actions of the family room - covered porch - nook - kitchen zone. Notice the raised hearth fireplace, the wood boxes, the sliding glass doors, built-in bar, and the kitchen pass-thru. Adding to the charm of the family room is its high ceiling. From the second floor hall one can look down and observe the activities below.

A Tudor adaptation with unique appeal and interesting living patterns. The main, two-story section of this house is flanked by two, one-story wings. Balancing the two-car garage is the living wing comprised of the formal living room and the informal family room.

Design S 2242

1,327 Sq. Ft. – First Floor/832 Sq. Ft. – Second Floor
35,315 Cu. Ft.

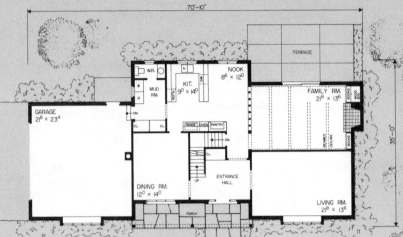

Design S 2108

1,188 Sq. Ft. – First Floor/720 Sq. Ft. – Second Floor/27,394 Cu. Ft.

Here is another variation of the two-story house. This design features a full two-story section flanked by one-story wings. Its livability is in no way restricted. In fact, what has resulted in this plan is an interesting and practical separation of functions to assure convenient living.

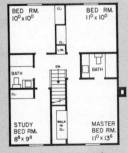

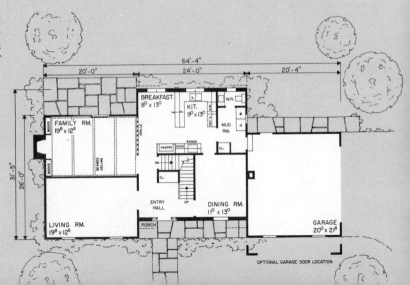

Design S 2190

1,221 Sq. Ft. – First Floor/884 Sq. Ft. – Second Floor
32,042 Cu. Ft.

Here is a modified Tudor adaptation with a popular interior floor plan. The covered front porch, the massive wood posts, the window treatment, and the patterned doors help set the character. There are interior features galore. The open planning of the formal living-dining areas results in a spacious atmosphere.

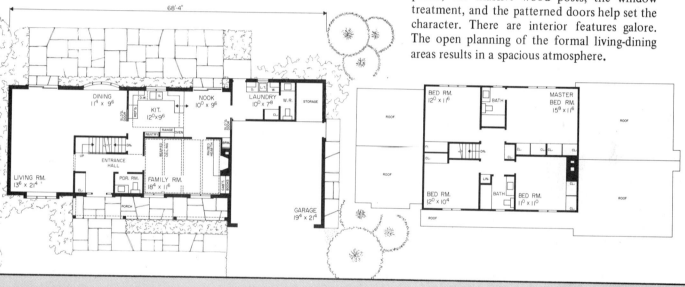

Design S 2188

1,440 Sq. Ft. – First Floor
1,280 Sq. Ft. – Second Floor
40,924 Cu. Ft.

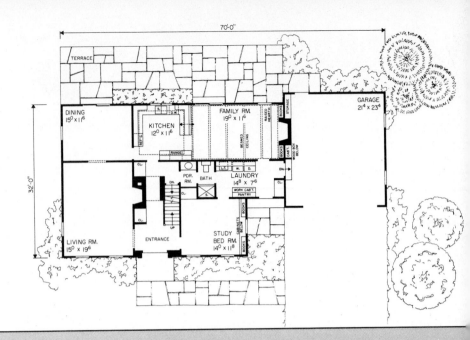

Design S 1814

1,471 Sq. Ft. – First Floor
1,052 Sq. Ft. – Second Floor
35,700 Cu. Ft.

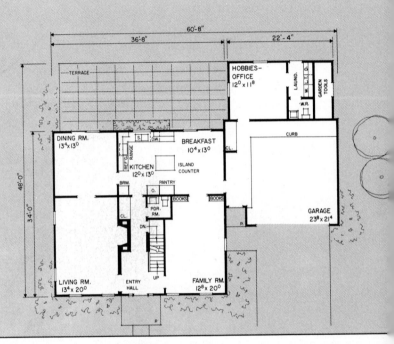

Design S 1266

1,374 Sq. Ft. – First Floor
1,094 Sq. Ft. – Second Floor
31,969 Cu. Ft.

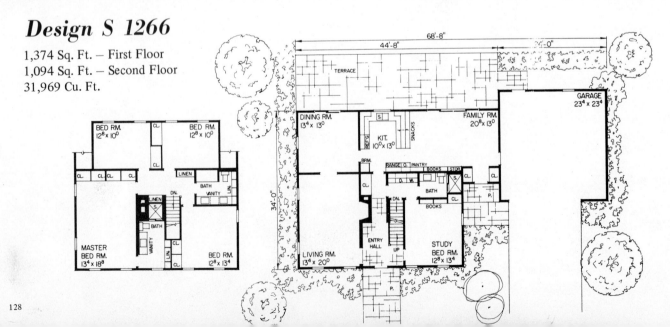

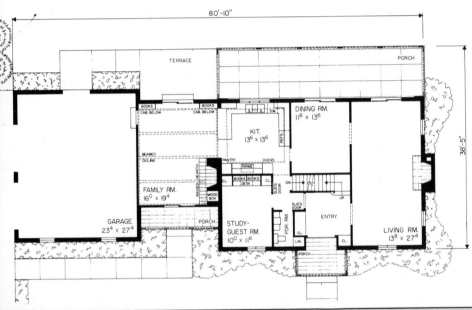

80'-10"

38'-5"

TERRACE   PORCH

BOOKS   BOOKS
CAB. BELOW   CAB. BELOW

DINING RM.
11⁶ x 13⁶

KIT.
13⁶ x 13⁶

BEAMED CEILING

PANTRY   OVENS
RANGE
BOOKS BOOKS   DESK
RAISED HEARTH

FAMILY RM.
16⁰ x 19⁴

WOOD BOX

GARAGE
23⁴ x 27⁴

PORCH

STUDY-GUEST RM.
10⁰ x 11⁶

PDR. RM.

CL.   LIN.

ENTRY

DN.   UP

LIVING RM.
13⁸ x 27⁴

PORCH

BED RM.
13⁶ x 13⁶

DRESS. RM.

MASTER BED RM.
17⁰ x 13⁶

BATH

CL.   CL.   CL.

DN.

HALL

BED RM.
10⁰ x 11²

LINEN
BATH   PDR. RM.

BED RM.
13⁰ x 13⁶

Design S 2222

1,485 Sq. Ft. — First Floor
1,175 Sq. Ft. — Second Floor
45,500 Cu. Ft.

88'-10"

47'-2"

BRICK TERRACE

STORAGE
9⁶ x 10⁰

LAUND.   W. R.

NOOK
8⁶ x 13⁶

KIT.
10⁰ x 13⁶

DINING RM.
13⁰ x 13⁶

CHINA

BEAMED CEILING

OVEN   RANGE   PANTRY   DESK
BOOKS   BOOKS   BOOKS
CABINETS

RAISED HEARTH

FAMILY RM.
15⁸ x 23⁴

WOOD BOX

GARAGE
23⁴ x 21⁴

STUDY
11⁰ x 13⁶

PDR. RM.

ENTRANCE HALL

DN.

LIVING RM.
15⁶ x 27⁴

PORCH

BED RM.
10⁴ x 13⁶

BED RM.
13⁰ x 11⁰

BATH   BATH

DRESSING RM.

LINEN
CL. CL.   CL. CL.

VANITY

DN.

OPEN STAIR WELL
RAILING

STAIR HALL

BED RM.
15⁰ x 11⁰

MASTER BED RM.
15⁴ x 17⁸

Design S 2281

1,961 Sq. Ft. — First Floor
1,472 Sq. Ft. — Second Floor
49,974 Cu. Ft.

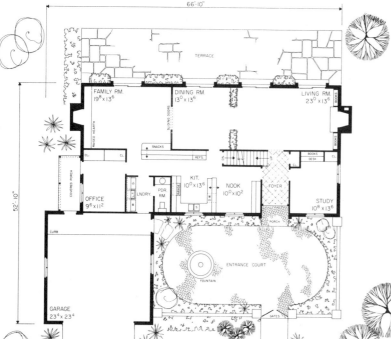

Design S 2326

1,674 Sq. Ft. — First Floor
1,107 Sq. Ft. — Second Floor
53,250 Cu. Ft.

Design S 2123

1,624 Sq. Ft. — First Floor/1,335 Sq. Ft. — Second Floor
42,728 Cu. Ft.

Inside there is close to 3,000 square feet of uniquely planned floor area. The spacious, well-lighted entry has, of course, a high sloping ceiling. A second floor balcony looks down from above. This area features two walk-in closets. Between the dining and living rooms is a thru fireplace which may be enjoyed from either room. Between the garage and the family room is the laundry and the compartmented powder room. The second floor ceilings slope and, consequently, add to the feeling of spaciousness.

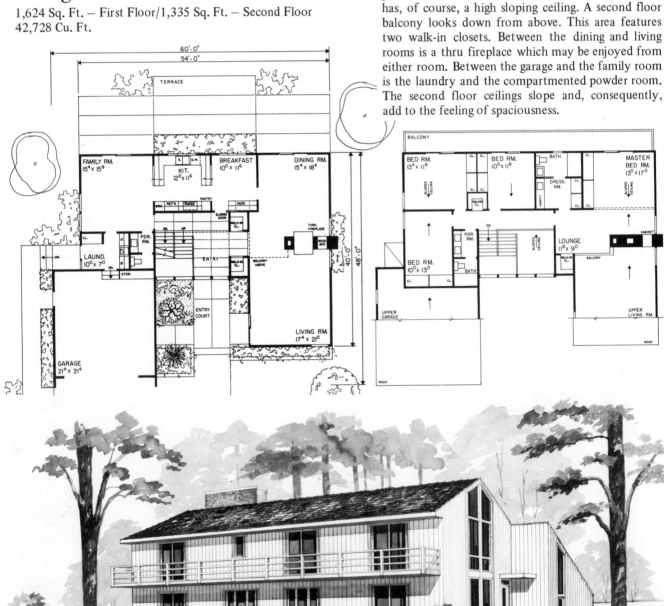

A contemporary adaptation of the design found on page 115. A comparison of these elevations offers an excellent study in the comparative appeal of traditional and contemporary facades. What is your preference? Should you wish to build without a basement the construction blueprints for this particular design show details for non-basement construction. Note how the optional non-basement plan locates the washer and dryer in the powder room. The L shape of living and dining rooms results in extra spaciousness, flexible furniture placement.

Design S 1908

1,122 Sq. Ft. – First Floor/896 Sq. Ft. – Second Floor
27,064 Cu. Ft.

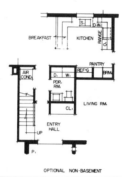

OPTIONAL NON-BASEMENT

Contemporary architecture can have its sedate adaptations of traditional forms. Here a Mansard roof configuration accompanies glass and masonry wall masses to produce a truly dramatic two-story. Projecting the one-story wing to the front provides an extra measure of appeal. Trellis work results in a partially covered walk to the front door. Inside, wonderful livability. List the features.

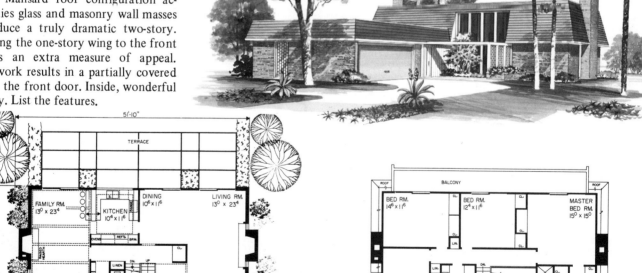

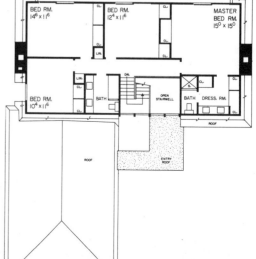

Design S 2187

1,435 Sq. Ft. – First Floor
1,152 Sq. Ft. – Second Floor
35,919 Cu. Ft.

Design S 2309 1,719 Sq. Ft. – First Floor/456 Sq. Ft. – Second Floor/22,200 Cu. Ft.

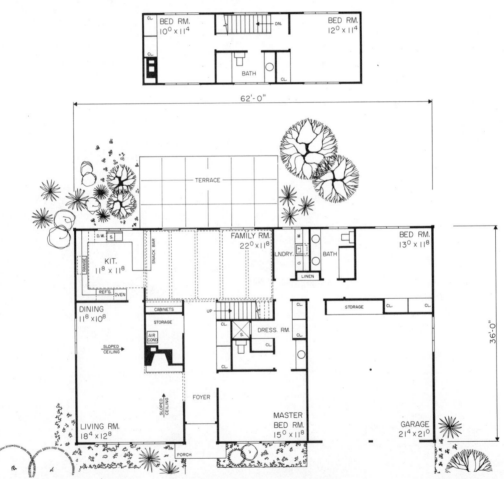

Here's proof that the simple rectangle (which is relatively economical to build, naturally) can, when properly planned, result in unique living patterns. The exterior can be exceedingly appealing, too. Study the floor plan carefully. The efficiency of the kitchen could hardly be improved upon. It is strategically located to serve the formal dining room, the family room, and even the rear terrace. The sleeping facilities are arranged in a most interesting manner. The master bedroom with its attached bath and dressing room enjoys a full measure of privacy on the first floor. A second bedroom is also on this floor and has a full bath nearby. Then, upstairs there are two more bedrooms. Don't miss the laundry, the snack bar, the beamed ceiling, or the sliding glass doors.

Here is a contemporary Mansard roof adaptation that is dramatic, indeed. Because of its simplicity it will not fail to elicit its full measure of acclaim. The vertical 1 x 3 inch battens and the glass panels add a distinctive note. The unique appeal of this design continues to be apparent on the inside as well. The center entrance hall effectively routes traffic. To the right is the kitchen-laundry area. To the left, the well-lighted open stairwell to the second floor. At the top of the stairs you can look over the balcony railing down into a portion of the living room. In addition to the formal living and dining rooms (which function togethther), there is the large beamed ceiling-ed family room. Note the bar, game storage, and sliding glass doors to terrace. Outstanding livability!

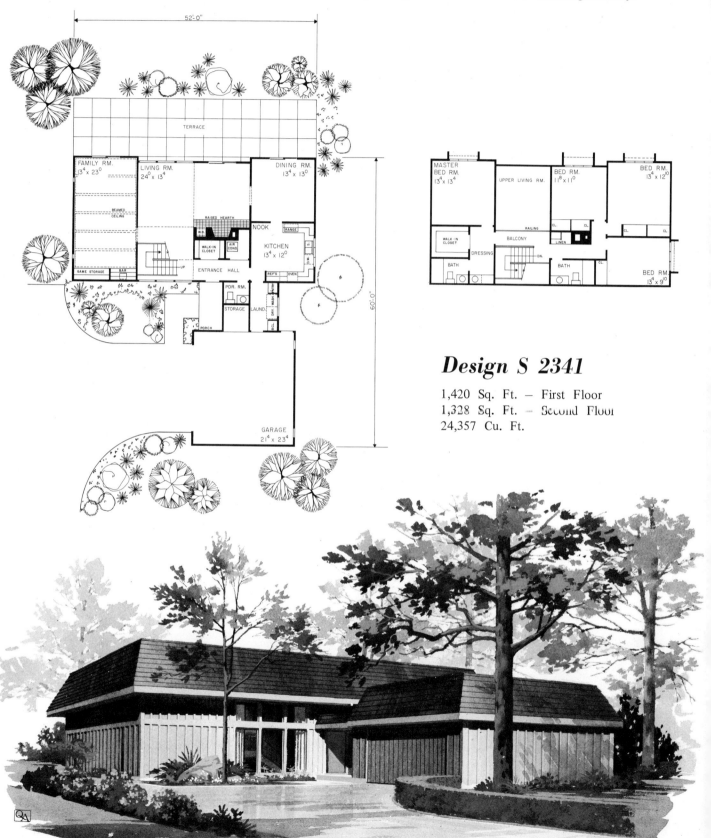

Design S 2341

1,420 Sq. Ft. — First Floor
1,328 Sq. Ft. — Second Floor
24,357 Cu. Ft.

Design S 2151

991 Sq. Ft. – First Floor
952 Sq. Ft. – Second Floor
28,964 Cu. Ft.

Here are two distinctive designs with the same basic floor plan. Whether you order blueprints for the Tudor design, S 2151, above, or the Farmhouse design, S 2150, below, you will receive details for both the four and five bedroom, versions. Note laundry, powder room, beamed ceiling, separate dining room.

OPTIONAL 4 BEDROOM PLAN

Design S 2150

991 Sq. Ft. – First Floor
952 Sq. Ft. – Second Floor
27,850 Cu. Ft.

Design S 1956

990 Sq. Ft. – First Floor
728 Sq. Ft. – Second Floor
23,703 Cu. Ft.

Even a modest house can function like a mansion. The large family will spend much time in the beamed ceiling family room. When doing so, there are still the living, dining, and four bedrooms ready to serve. Note three bedroom plan.

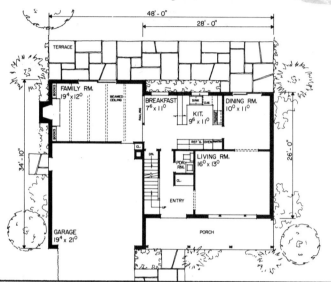

OPTIONAL 3 BEDROOM PLAN

Design S 1361

965 Sq. Ft. – First Floor
740 Sq. Ft. – Second Floor
23,346 Cu. Ft.

An abundance of livability in a charming traditional adaptation which will be most economical to build. Count the features, they are numerous. Study the layout. It is outstanding. All the elements are present in this design for fine family living. Three bedrooms, 2½ baths, family room, dining room, and even a first floor laundry.

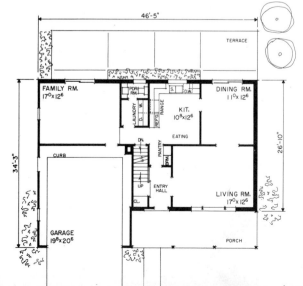

137

Design S 1783
2,412 Sq. Ft. — First Floor/640 Sq. Ft. — Second Floor/36,026 Cu. Ft.

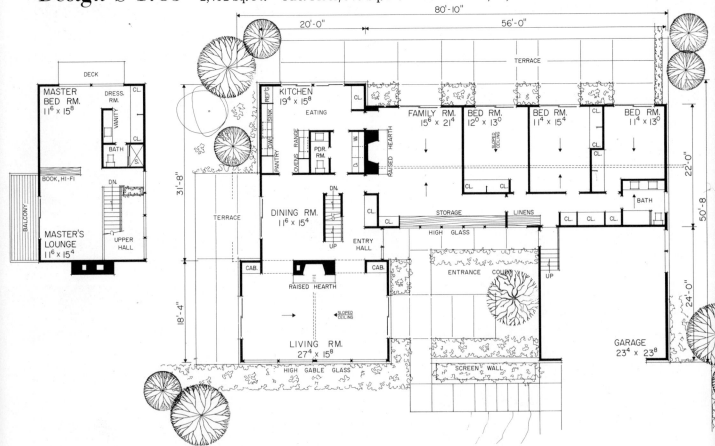

Large families, take notice! Here is an impressive contemporary that is not only going to be fun to live in, but to look at, as well. Contributing to the appeal of this design are the interesting roof levels, their exposed rafters and wide overhangs. A big entrance court, screened from the street by a masonry wall, heightens the drama of the front exterior. The 27 foot living room is captivating, indeed. It can function through sliding glass doors, with either the front court or the side terrace. Eating patterns can be quite flexible with the extra space in the kitchen, a formal dining room, and also a dining terrace. Don't miss sloping ceilings. The rear terrace is accessible from kitchen, family room, and each of the three first floor bedrooms. Upstairs, there is the wonderful bedroom suite.

Traditional & Contemporary
Multi - Level Homes

Design S 2219
1,464 Sq. Ft. — Upper Level/728 Sq. Ft. — Lower Level/21,640 Cu. Ft.

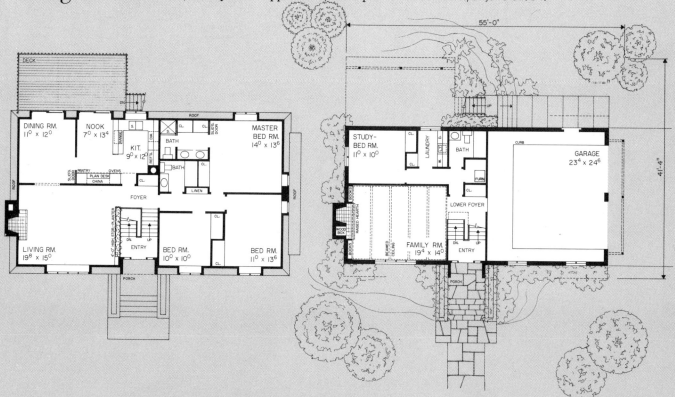

The popular and formal French Mansard roof has been adapted here to an outstanding bi-level design. Frequently referred to as a split-foyer design, the upper level is the main living level. It is a complete living unit. Here, it functions exceedingly well with a three

bedroom, two bath sleeping zone; a sizeable, quiet living zone; an efficient work center and eating zone. The eating zone is comprised of both formal and informal rooms that are directly accessible through sliding glass doors to the rear deck. The lower level

provides the necessary area for the ever popular family room; an extra bedroom or study; a laundry with third bath nearby; a large two-car garage. Note the two fireplaces. One has a raised hearth flanked by books. Observe built-in planter.

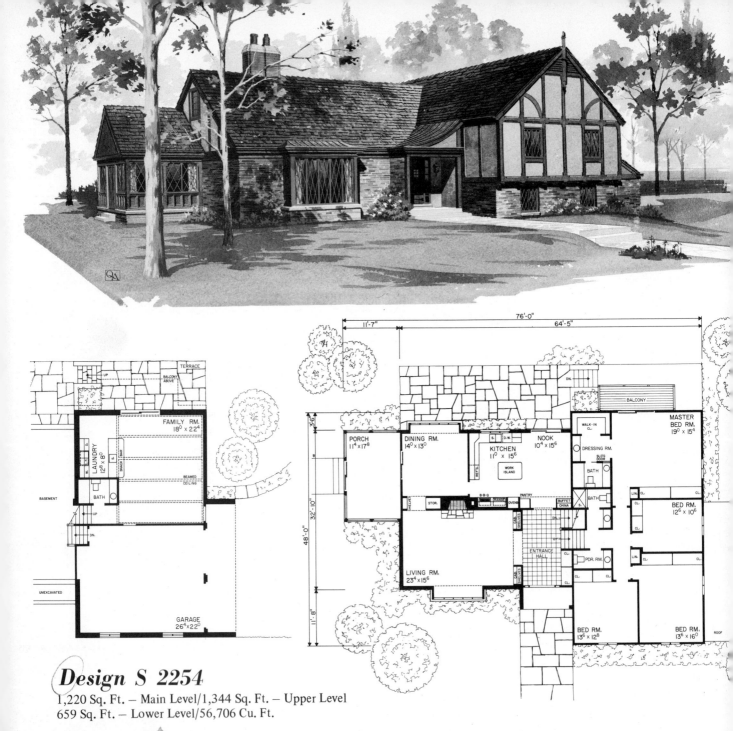

Design S 2254

1,220 Sq. Ft. — Main Level/1,344 Sq. Ft. — Upper Level
659 Sq. Ft. — Lower Level/56,706 Cu. Ft.

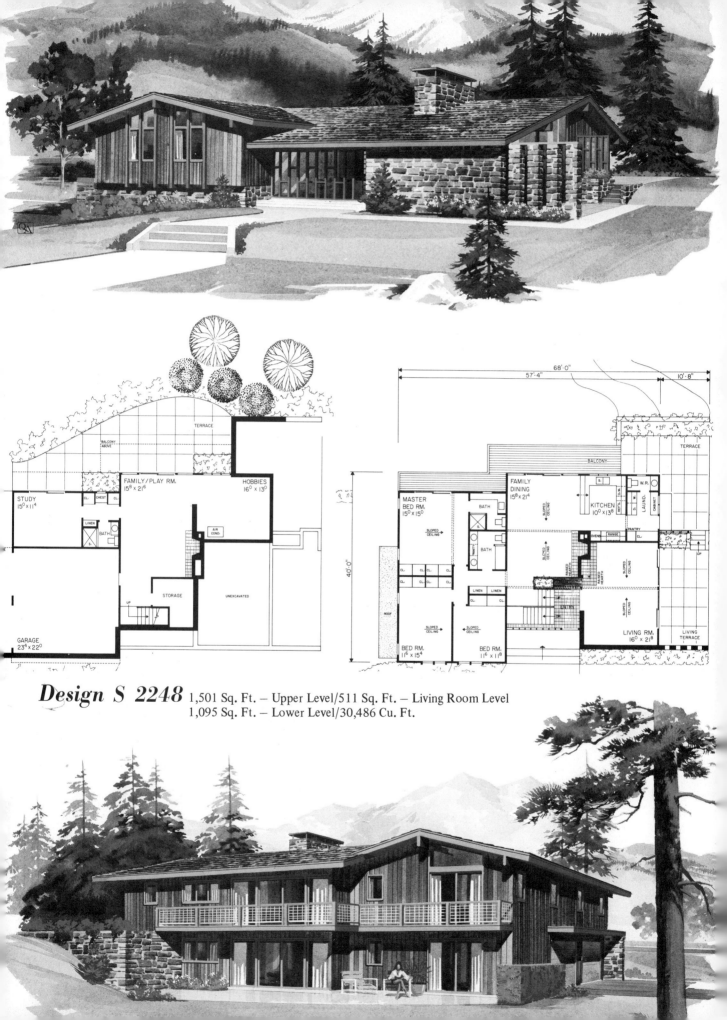

Design S 2248 1,501 Sq. Ft. — Upper Level/511 Sq. Ft. — Living Room Level
1,095 Sq. Ft. — Lower Level/30,486 Cu. Ft.

Floor plan labels (upper level):
TERRACE
BALCONY ABOVE
STUDY 15⁰ x 11⁴
FAMILY/PLAY RM. 15⁸ x 21⁶
HOBBIES 16⁰ x 13⁰
LINEN
BATH
AIR COND.
STORAGE
UNEXCAVATED
UP
GARAGE 23⁴ x 22⁰
CL.
CHEST
CL.
S.

Floor plan labels (living room level):
68'-0"
57'-4"
10'-8"
40'-0"
TERRACE
BALCONY
MASTER BED RM. 15⁰ x 15⁰
FAMILY DINING 15⁸ x 21⁴
KITCHEN 10⁰ x 13⁸
LAUND.
W.R.
CABINET
BATH
BATH
SLOPED CEILING
RAISED HEARTH
PANTRY
OVEN
RANGE
ROOF
SLOPED CEILING
LINEN LINEN
CL.
ENTRY
LIVING RM. 16⁰ x 21⁸
LIVING TERRACE
BED RM. 11⁶ x 15⁴
BED RM. 11⁶ x 11⁸
SLOPED CEILING
CL.
VANITY
UP

Design S 1927
1,272 Sq. Ft. — Main Level
960 Sq. Ft. — Upper Level/936 Sq. Ft. — Lower Level/36,815 Cu. Ft.

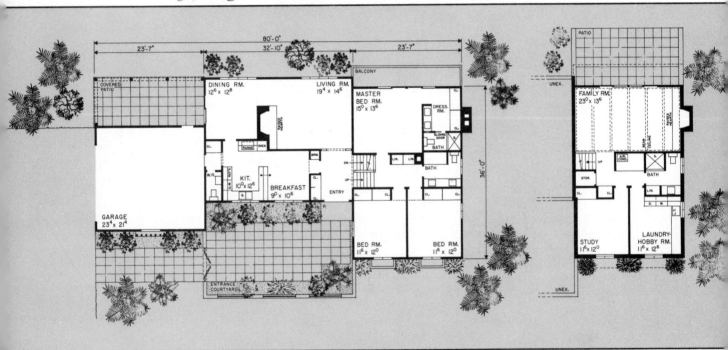

Design S 2186
915 Sq. Ft. — Main Level
960 Sq. Ft. — Upper Level/960 Sq. Ft. — Lower Level/33,130 Cu. Ft.

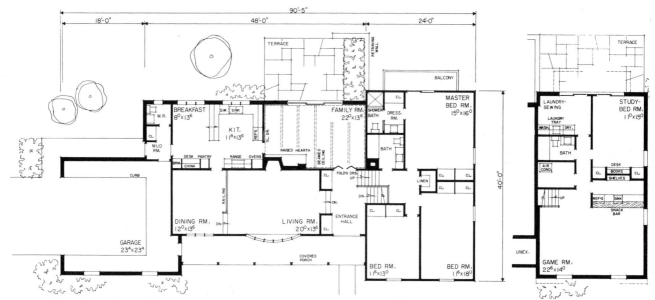

Design S 2143

832 Sq. Ft. — Main Level/864 Sq. Ft. — Upper Level
864 Sq. Ft. — Lower Level/27,473 Cu. Ft.

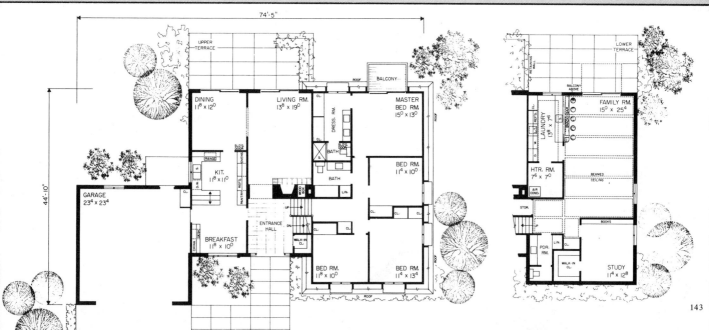

143

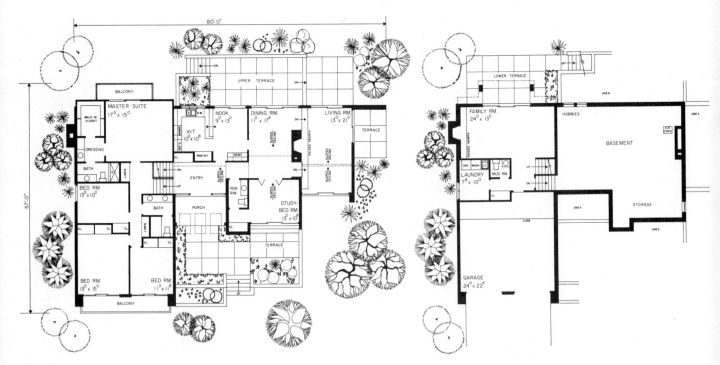

Design S 2516

1,183 Sq. Ft. – Main Level / 1,248 Sq. Ft. – Upper Level / 607 Sq. Ft. – Lower Level / 41,775 Cu. Ft.

Your family will certainly have fun living in this multi-level home with its pleasingly contemporary exterior. As is easily discernible from a quick glance at the exterior and plan, this home offers excellent indoor-outdoor living patterns. Notice how the majority of the rooms function through sliding glass doors with the outside balconies and terraces. Delightfully large glass areas and sloping ceilings help foster a spacious interior. The end living room with its raised hearth fireplace and adjacent terraces will be a most enjoyable room. The master suite is large and has a dressing area, private bath, walk-in closet, and outdoor balcony. In addition to the lower level family room there is the basement level. This is a generous area for hobbies and bulk storage. Locate pool table here.

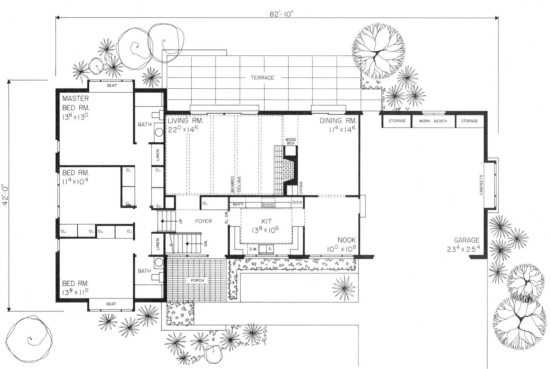

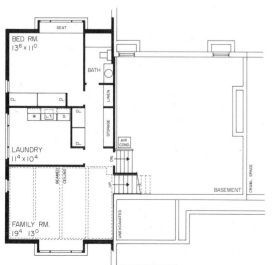

Design S 2314

974 Sq. Ft. – Main Level / 826 Sq. Ft. – Upper Level
832 Sq. Ft. – Lower Level / 32,063 Cu. Ft.

Similar in character to its split-level companion on the opposing page, this contemporary design's living patterns are, interestingly enough, quite different. Living patterns flow to the rear with both the living and dining rooms functioning through sliding glass doors with the big terrace. Separating these two rooms is the attractive fireplace. A handy wood box is at one end; a convenient china closet at the other. The upper level has three bedrooms, two baths and lots of closets. The lower level highlights a fourth bedroom, a large laundry room and beamed ceilinged family room. A basement level permits the development of additional recreational and hobby space.

Design S 1778

1,344 Sq. Ft. — Upper Level
768 Sq. Ft. — Lower Level
22,266 Cu. Ft.

Interesting? You bet it is. The low-pitched, wide overhanging roof, the vertical siding, and the dramatic glass areas give the facade of this contemporary bi-level house an appearance all its own. This type of house provides an outstanding return on your construction dollar.

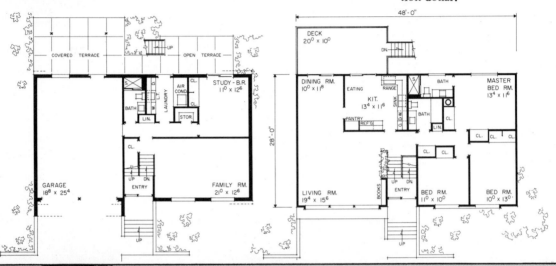

Design S 1220

1,456 Sq. Ft. — Upper Level
862 Sq. Ft. — Lower Level
22,563 Cu. Ft.

This fresh, contemporary exterior sets the stage for exceptional livability. Measuring only 52 feet across the front, this bi-level home offers the large family outstanding features. Whether called upon to function as a four or five bedroom home, there is plenty of space in which to move around. Note both balconies.

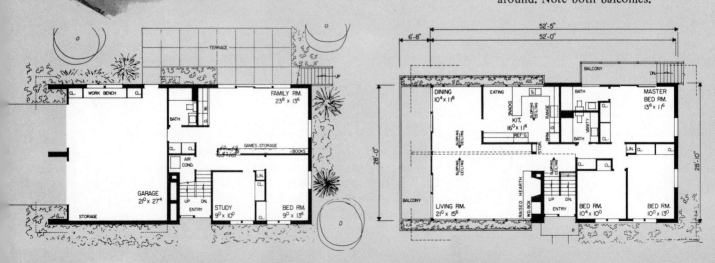

Design S 1310

1,040 Sq. Ft. — Upper Level
694 Sq. Ft. — Lower Level
17,755 Cu. Ft.

An interesting version of the ever-popular two-story. If you want something new in low-cost living patterns, this two-level home may be just the right one for you. This economically built 40' x 26' basic rectangle incorporates the oversized garage and the huge family room on the first level.

Design S 1704

1,498 Sq. Ft. — Upper Level
870 Sq. Ft. — Lower Level
23,882 Cu. Ft.

The bi-level concept of living is becoming popular. This is understandable, for it represents a fine way in which to gain a maximum amount of extra livable area beneath the basic floor plan.

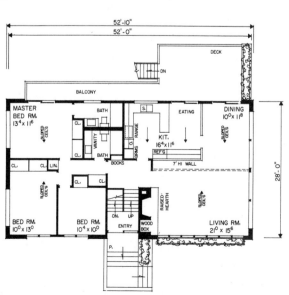

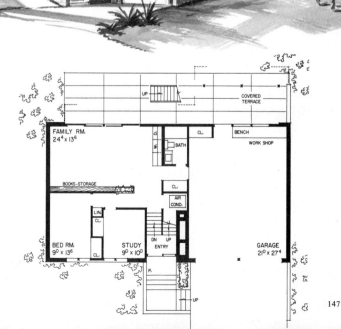

147

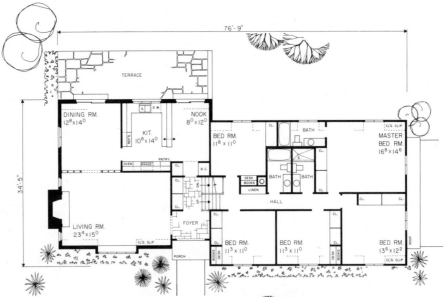

Design S 2331

988 Sq. Ft. — Main Level
1,260 Sq. Ft. — Upper Level
525 Sq. Ft. — Lower Level
35,486 Cu. Ft.

A picture to behold! The charm of this gracious Tudor adaptation will make it a sightseers favorite wherever built. The quarried stone (make it brick, if you prefer), the timber work, the stucco, the expanses of roof, the window treatment, and the stolid double front doors are features which combine to achieve a truly delightful exterior. The interior of this tri-level is well-zoned to deliver excellent living patterns. There is the formal living room and the informal family room. Flanking the U-shaped work center is the separate dining room and the breakfast nook. The upper level provides the large family with five bedrooms and three full baths. Don't miss the laundry/sewing/hobby room.

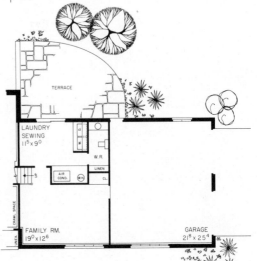

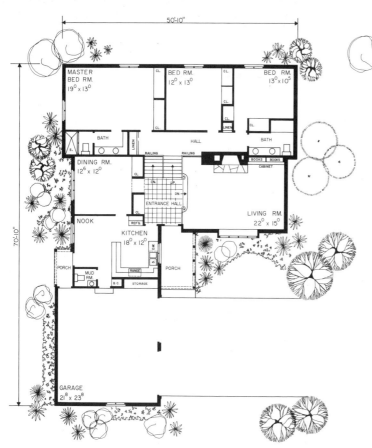

This English flavored tri-level design may be built on a flat site. Its configuration permits a flexible orientation on the site with either the garage doors or the front door facing the street. The interior offers a unique and practical floor plan layout. Flanking the spacious entrance hall is the cozy, sunken living room and the formal dining room. Looking out upon the front porch is the kitchen with its adjacent nook. A mud room is strategically located just inside the door from the garage. Opposite the front door are two flights of stairs. One leads to the upper level with its three bedrooms and two baths. The other leads to the lower level. Here is a fourth bedroom, third bathroom, a big beamed ceiling family room, a hobby room, and a laundry. A real winner for family living.

Design S 2354

936 Sq. Ft. – Main Level / 971 Sq. Ft.   Upper Level / 971 Sq. Ft. – Lower Level / 34,561 Cu. Ft.

Design S 2171

795 Sq. Ft. — Main Level
912 Sq. Ft. — Upper Level
335 Sq. Ft. — Lower Level
33,243 Cu. Ft.

This English Tudor split-level adaptation has much in common with its counterpart on the opposing page. While some 400 square feet smaller it offers a number of distinguishing features. Observe the living room and family room fireplaces.

Here is a fine marriage of a Tudor exterior with a split-level plan. The result is delightful to look at and a joy to live in. The features are almost endless. Try listing them.

Design S 2137

987 Sq. Ft. – Main Level
1,043 Sq. Ft. – Upper Level
463 Sq. Ft. – Lower Level
29,382 Cu. Ft.

Tudor design adapts to split-level living. The result is an unique charm for all to remember. As for the livability, the happy occupants of this tri-level home will experience wonderful living patterns. A covered porch protects, and adds charm to front entry.

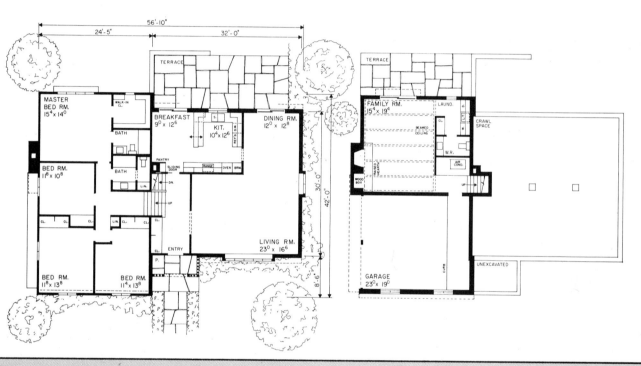

Design S 2243

1,274 Sq. Ft. – Main Level/960 Sq. Ft. – Upper Level/936 Sq. Ft. – Lower Level
42,478 Cu. Ft.

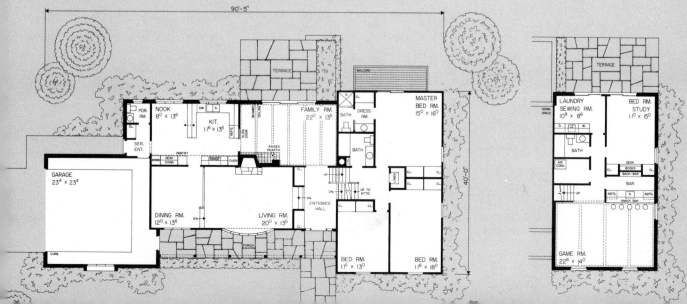

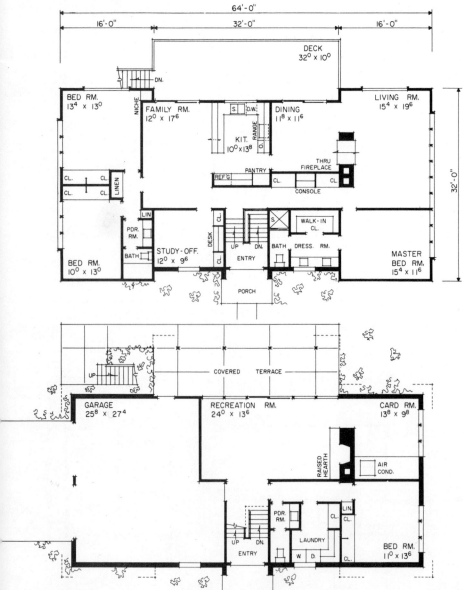

Upper level floor plan:
64'-0"
16'-0" | 32'-0" | 16'-0"
32'-0"

DECK
32⁰ x 10⁰

BED RM.
13⁴ x 13⁰

NICHE

FAMILY RM.
12⁰ x 17⁶

KIT.
10⁰ x 13⁸

S. D.W.
RANGE

DINING
11⁸ x 11⁶

LIVING RM.
15⁴ x 19⁶

DN.

CL. CL.
CL. CL.
LINEN

REF'G.
PANTRY
CONSOLE
CL.

THRU
FIREPLACE

LIN
PDR. RM.
BATH

STUDY - OFF.
12⁰ x 9⁶

DESK
CL.
CL.

UP DN.

S.
WALK - IN
CL.

BATH DRESS. RM.

ENTRY

BED RM.
10⁰ x 13⁰

MASTER
BED RM.
15⁴ x 11⁶

PORCH

Lower level floor plan:

UP

COVERED TERRACE

GARAGE
25⁸ x 27⁴

RECREATION RM.
24⁰ x 13⁶

CARD RM.
13⁸ x 9⁸

RAISED
HEARTH

AIR
COND.

PDR.
RM.

LIN
CL.

CL.

UP DN.

LAUNDRY

ENTRY

W. D.

BED RM.
11⁰ x 13⁶

Design S 1782

1,920 Sq. Ft.—Upper Level
1,036 Sq. Ft.—Lower Level
30,672 Cu. Ft.

Bi-level living is depicted here in a
most impressive fashion. Its facade
is highlighted by delightful symmetry characterized by the brick piers,
the two sets of windows, and the
projecting bays of vertical siding.
Study the unique, yet practical,
manner in which the various areas
of the upper level function. Observe
the children's sleeping area and how
it is separated from the parent's
master bedroom suite. Note the locations of the informal and formal
living areas in relation to these two
sleeping areas. Study the lower level
with its recreation room, card room
laundry and extra bedroom.

Design S 1842

1,747 Sq. Ft.—Upper Level
937 Sq. Ft.—Lower Level
27,212 Cu. Ft.

If it is space you are after, plus exquisite design, with both put together and offered in a refreshing package, you have found what you've been looking for. From the outstanding laundry room of the lower level to the outdoor balcony of the master bedroom this home is filled with features. Start listing them with the 27 foot storage wall in the garage. Continue with the 31 foot family room, the study, the exceptional kitchen, the raised hearth fireplace, the built-in china cabinets, the barbecue unit, the dressing room with vanity, the breakfast room, and the spacious deck.

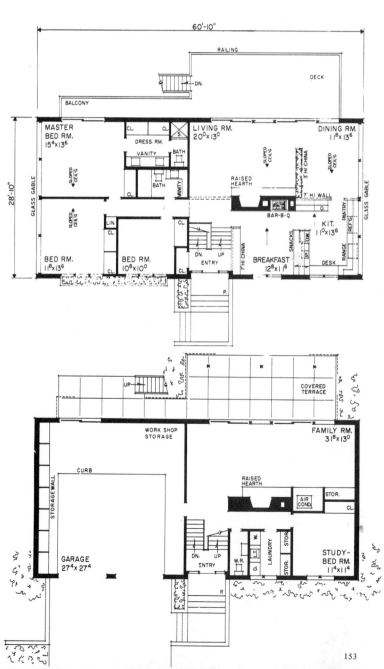

Design S 3151 1,209 Sq. Ft. — Main Level/899 Sq. Ft. — Upper Level/912 Sq. Ft. — Lower Level/30,620 Cu. Ft.

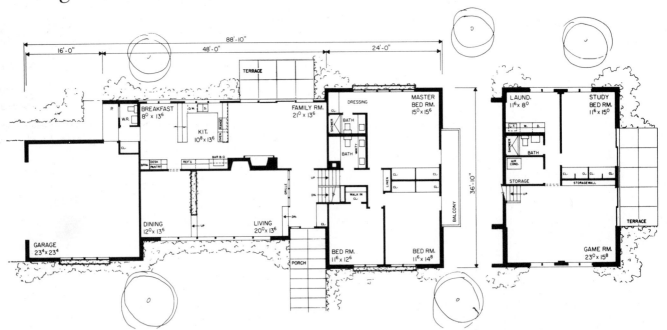

Split-level living can be great fun. And it certainly will be for the occupants of this impressive house. First and foremost, you and your family will appreciate the practical zoning. The upper level is the quiet sleeping level. List the features. They are many. The main level is zoned for both formal and informal living. Don't miss the sunken living room or the twin fireplaces. The lower level provides that extra measure of livability.

Design S 1298 1,578 Sq. Ft. – Main Level/1,184 Sq. Ft. – Lower Level/26,720 Cu. Ft.

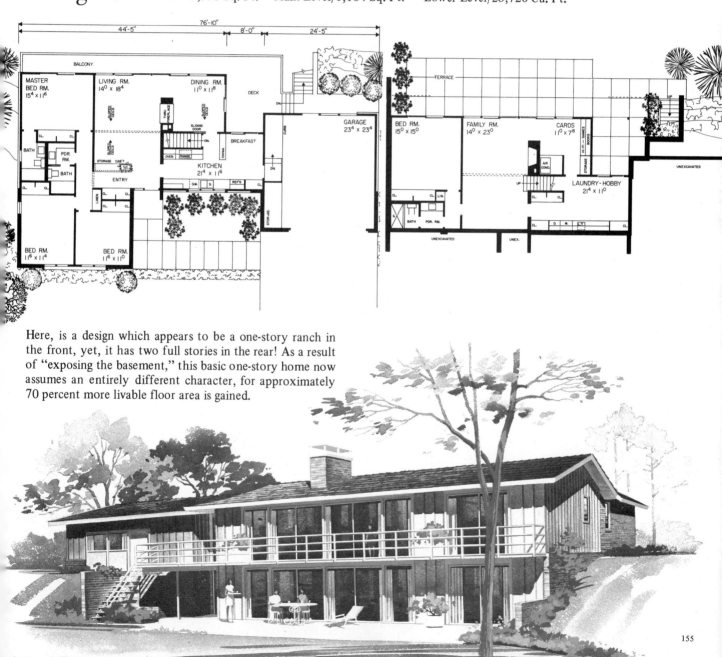

Here, is a design which appears to be a one-story ranch in the front, yet, it has two full stories in the rear! As a result of "exposing the basement," this basic one-story home now assumes an entirely different character, for approximately 70 percent more livable floor area is gained.

155

Design S 1358

576 Sq. Ft. – Main Level/672 Sq. Ft. – Upper Level
328 Sq. Ft. – Lower Level/20,784 Cu. Ft.

Have you been looking for a tri-level home with plenty of charm to build on your relatively narrow sloping building site? If so, look no further; for here is a home with loads of appeal and plenty of livability to go along with it.

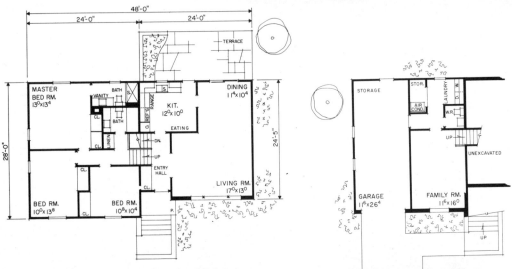

Design S 1230

728 Sq. Ft. – Main Level/792 Sq. Ft. – Upper Level
316 Sq. Ft. – Lower Level/728 Sq. Ft. –
Recreation Level/28,880 Cu. Ft.

A pleasingly traditional side-to-side split-level which features four distinct levels to service the activities of the active family. The gently sloping roofs have wide overhangs. A covered front porch extends clear across the main level wing.

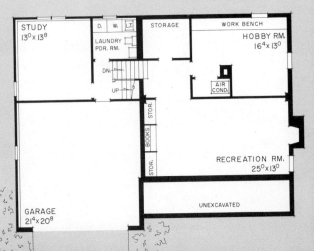

Design S 1981

784 Sq. Ft. – Main Level
912 Sq. Ft. – Upper Level
336 Sq. Ft. – Lower Level/26,618 Cu. Ft.

Have a relatively narrow building site? A restricted building budget? Or, would you just plain like a modest sized home, with loads of livability that can be built relatively economically and not use up a lot of property? Consider this!

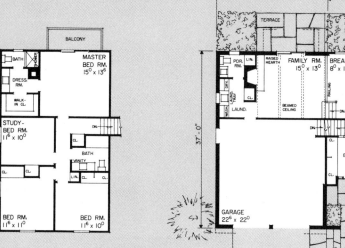

Design S 1771

942 Sq. Ft. – Main Level
1,010 Sq. Ft. – Upper Level
522 Sq. Ft. – Lower Level/26,024 Cu. Ft.

What are the features of this refreshing multi-level which you will like best? Well, it is hard to say, simply because there will be so many highlights contributing to your everyday, convenient living routine. Why not poll your family about its favorite features?

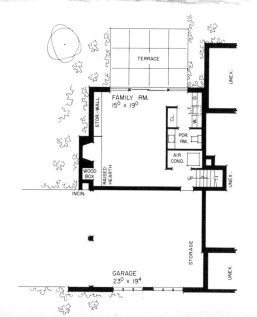

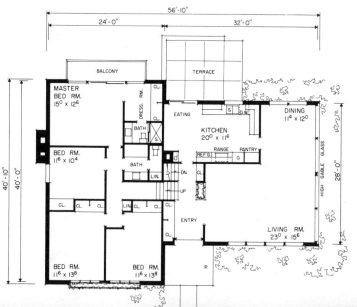

157

Here is an interesting home that has much to offer - both in the manner of exterior design and interior livability. Impressive areas of brick and vertical siding contrast effectively with appealing applications of glass. This interior is, indeed, spacious and forever conscious of the surrounding countryside. Notice how each of the major rooms functions through sliding glass doors with the outside. The living room and dining-kitchen area share one big terrace. The upper level bedrooms have their long balcony. And the lower level study (or fourth bedroom, if you wish) and family room have an equally long terrace. Observe the basement level, the sloping ceilings, the sunken kitchen area, the raised hearth fireplace, and all the various storage facilities. Don't miss the 3½ baths.

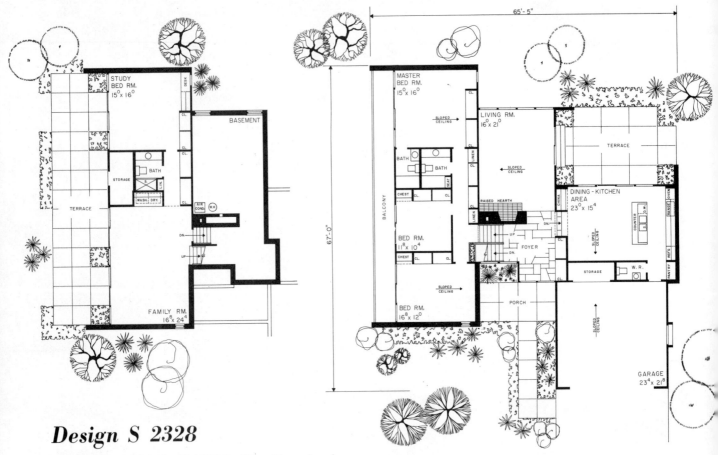

Design S 2328

1,036 Sq. Ft. — Main Level / 972 Sq. Ft. — Upper Level
972 Sq. Ft. — Lower Level / 36,877 Cu. Ft.

If you have been looking for a refreshing contemporary home with unique zoning which caters to the younger generation's activities, give this design much thought. The upper level, reached by passing through the bright and cheerful gallery, is for the teenage set.

Their own activities area is surrounded by four bedrooms and a vanity—bath—powder room area. Far removed is the parents' master bedroom zone on the main level. The children may pass from the family room directly to their own sleeping quarters, while the parents'

quarters are directly accessible from the living room. The projecting living room enjoys the use of both outdoor terraces. The U-shaped kitchen is but a step from the dining room and within reach of the snack bar. An outstanding kitchen in which to function.

Design S 2345

1,840 Sq. Ft. — Main Level
1,008 Sq. Ft. — Upper Level
38,260 Cu. Ft.

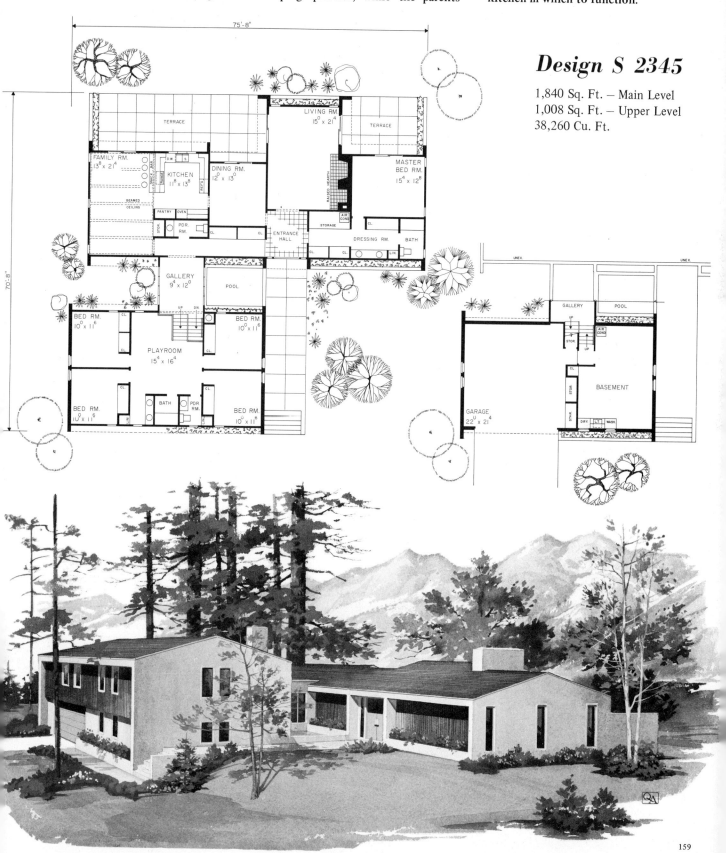

Tri-level living behind a charmingly proportioned traditional facade. A great low-budget home which will return plenty of livability.

Design S 1308

496 Sq. Ft. – Main Level/572 Sq. Ft. – Upper Level
537 Sq. Ft. – Lower Level/16,024 Cu. Ft.

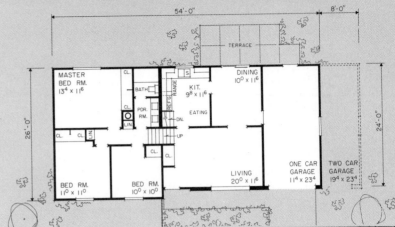

Design S 1850

1,456 Sq. Ft. – Upper Level/728 Sq. Ft. – Lower Level
23,850 Cu. Ft.

Often referred to as a split-foyer type of design, this bi-level will be an outstanding investment. A most economically built design.

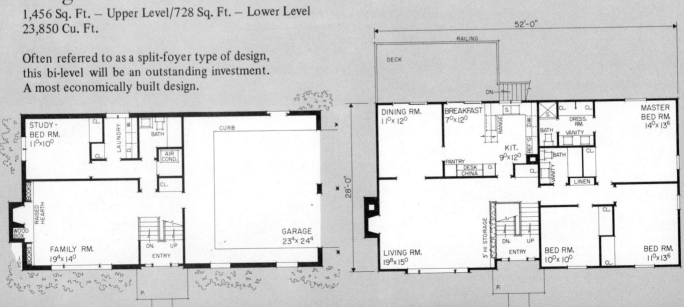

Design S 1210

1,248 Sq. Ft. – Upper Level/676 Sq. Ft. – Lower Level
19,812 Cu. Ft.

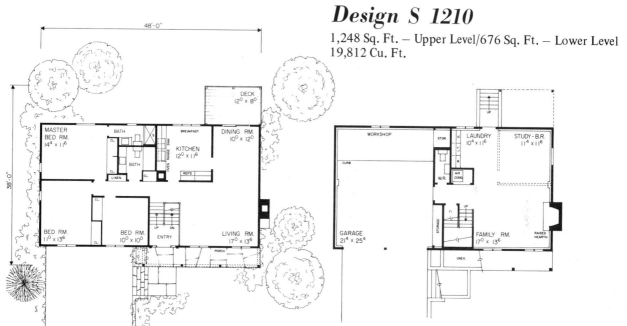

48'-0"

38'-0"

MASTER BED RM. 14⁴ x 11⁶

BATH

BATH

CL.

CL.

LINEN

CL.

DECK 12⁰ x 8⁰

BREAKFAST

DINING RM. 10⁰ x 12⁰

KITCHEN 12⁰ x 11⁶

OVEN RANGE SINK

REF'S

BED RM. 11⁰ x 13⁶

CL.

CL.

BED RM. 10⁰ x 10⁰

UP DN.

ENTRY

LIVING RM. 17 x 13⁶

PORCH

WORKSHOP

STOR.

CURB

W.R.

AIR COND.

LAUNDRY 10⁴ x 11⁶

STUDY - B.R. 11⁴ x 11⁶

UP

GARAGE 21⁴ x 25⁴

STORAGE

UP

FAMILY RM. 17 x 13⁶

UNEX.

RAISED HEARTH

Design S 1974   1,680 Sq. Ft. — Upper Level/1,344 Sq. Ft. — Lower Level/34,186 Cu. Ft.

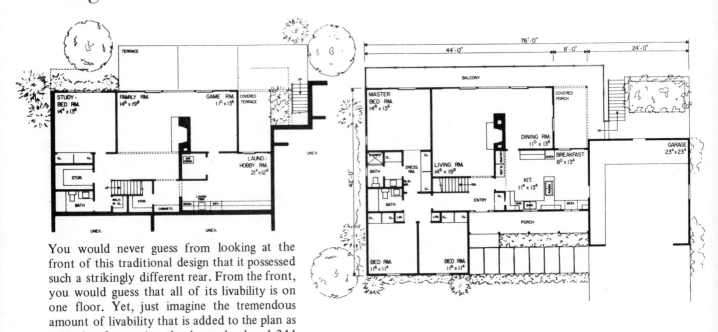

You would never guess from looking at the front of this traditional design that it possessed such a strikingly different rear. From the front, you would guess that all of its livability is on one floor. Yet, just imagine the tremendous amount of livability that is added to the plan as a result of exposing the lower level — 1,344 square feet of it. Living in this hillside house will mean fun. Obviously, most popular spot will be the balcony.

Design S 2218 889 Sq. Ft. – Main Level/960 Sq. Ft. – Upper Level/936 Sq. Ft. – Lower Level/33,865 Cu. Ft.

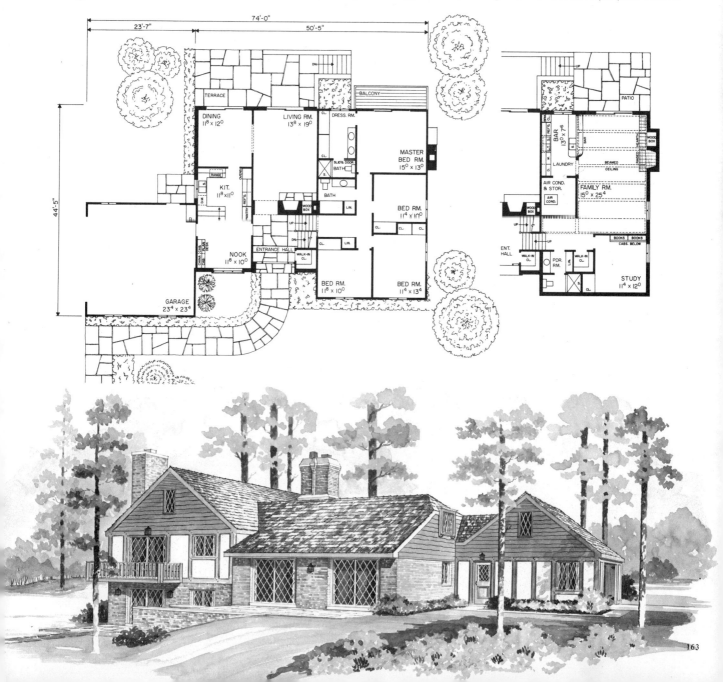

Design S 1977

896 Sq. Ft.—Main Level
884 Sq. Ft.—Upper Level
896 Sq. Ft.—Lower Level
36,718 Cu. Ft.

This split-level with its impressive two-story center portion flanked by a projecting living wing on one side and a two-car garage on the other side, still maintains that very desirable ground-hugging quality. Built entirely of frame with narrow horizontal siding (brick veneer could be substituted), this home will sparkle with a New England flavor. Upon passing through the double front doors, you'll be impressed by orderly flow of traffic. You'll go up to the sleeping zone; down to the hobby/recreation level; straight ahead to the kitchen/eating area; left to the quiet living room. Noteworthy are the extra bath, bedroom, and beamed ceiling family room with fireplace on lower level.

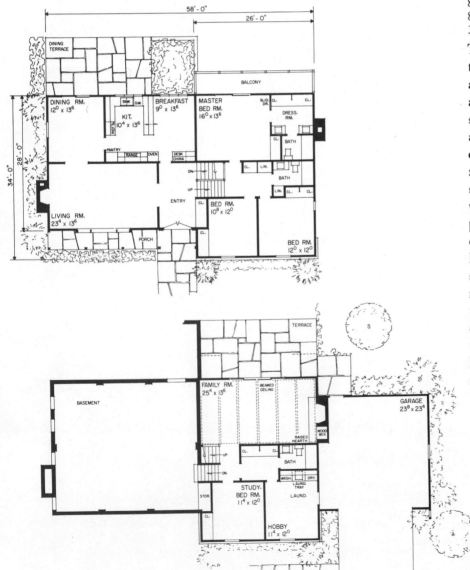

Design S 2125

728 Sq. Ft.—Main Level
672 Sq. Ft.—Upper Level
656 Sq. Ft.—Lower Level
28,315 Cu. Ft.

This four level traditional home has a long list of features to recommend it. First of all it is real beauty to look at. The windows, the shutters, the doorway, the horizontal siding with corner boards, and the stone work all go together with great proportion to project and image of design excellence. Inside, the livability is outstanding for such a modest home. There are three bedrooms, plus a study (make it the fourth bedroom if you wish); two full baths and a wash room; a fine kitchen with eating space; a spacious formal living and dining area; a big, all-purpose family room. Then there are such highlights as the fireplace, the laundry, and the sliding glass doors.

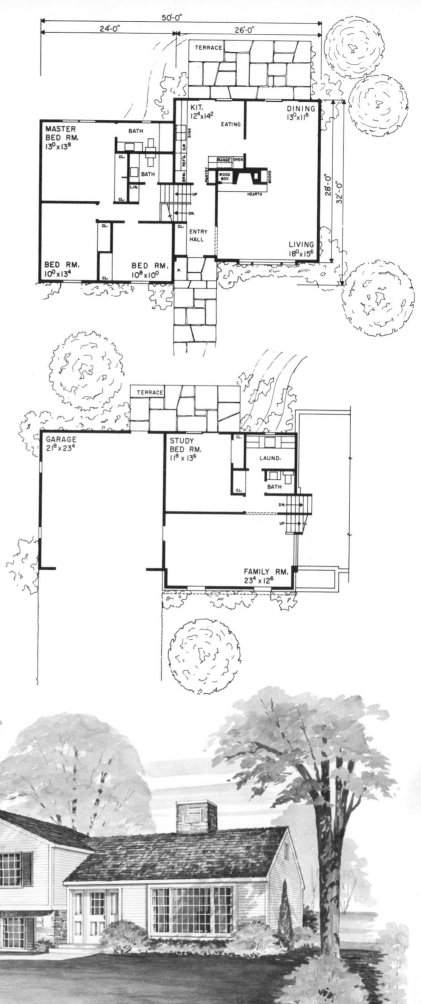

Design S 1930

947 Sq. Ft. — Main Level/768 Sq. Ft. — Upper Level
740 Sq. Ft. — Lower Level/25,906 Cu. Ft.

Design S 1795

804 Sq. Ft. — Main Level/672 Sq. Ft. — Upper Level
624 Sq. Ft. — Lower Level/26,615 Cu. Ft.

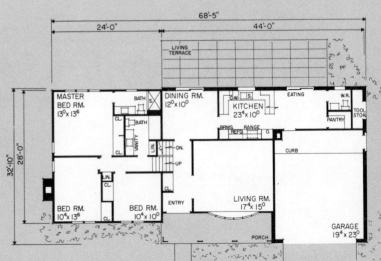

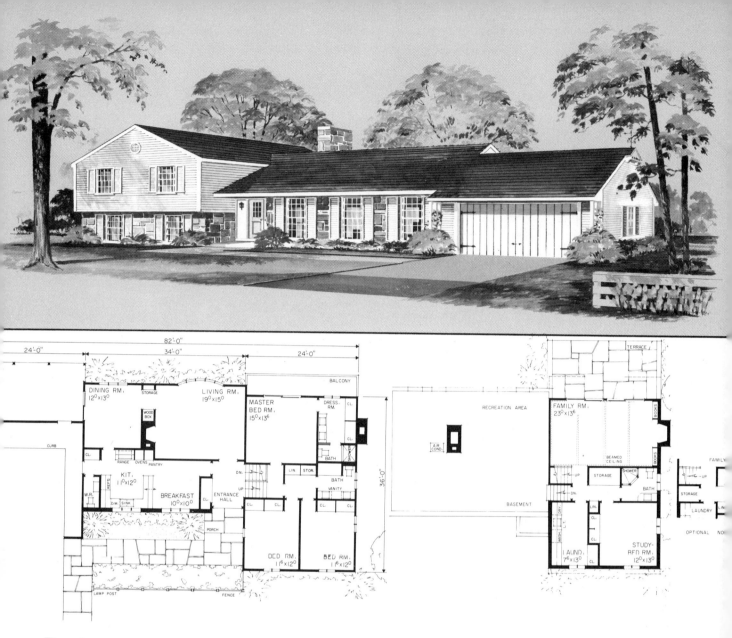

Design S 1935 904 Sq. Ft. — Main Level/864 Sq. Ft. — Upper Level/840 Sq. Ft. — Lower Level/26,745 Cu. Ft.

Three Stacked Levels Of Livability

Design S 2511

1,043 Sq. Ft. Main Level / 703 Sq. Ft. — Upper Level
794 Sq. Ft. — Lower Level / 30,528 Cu. Ft.

Distinctive and newly fashioned, this geometric hillside home offers interesting living patterns. Its interior is as individualistic as its exterior. The main living level is delightfully planned with the efficient kitchen easily serving the snack bar and the dining room. The gathering room has a high ceiling and looks up at the upper level balcony. An angular deck provides the gathering and dining rooms with their outdoor living area. A study with an adjacent full bath, provides the main level with an extra measure of living pattern flexibility. It has its own quiet outdoor balcony. Upstairs, a bunk room, a bedroom, and full bath. Also, there is an exciting view through the gathering room windows. On the lower level an optional sleeping facility, the family's all-purpose activities room, a hobby room, and another full bath.

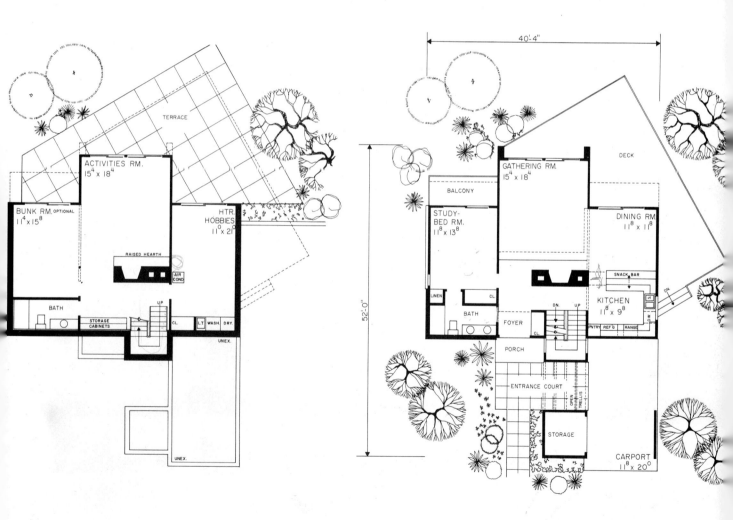

Design S 1812 — 1,726 Sq. Ft. — Upper Level/1,320 Sq. Ft. — Lower Level/30,142 Cu. Ft.

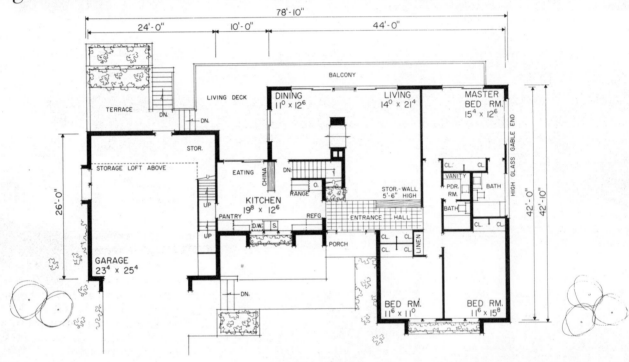

A home with two faces. The street view of this contemporary design presents a most pleasingly formal facade. The wide overhanging roof, the projecting masonry piers, the attractive glass treatment, and the recessed front entrance all go together to form a perfectly delightful image. The rear terrace view is a picture of informality. The upper level outdoor balcony, overhanging the sweeping lower level terrace, will make summer entertaining an occasion to look forward to. The balcony gives way to the spacious deck which will be an ideal spot on which to sun-bathe or dine. The plan is interesting, indeed. A two-way fireplace separates the big living-dining area. Observe the work center; study the lower level layout. Be sure to note the extra bedroom.

Vacation Homes

Design S 1432

1,512 Sq. Ft. – First Floor
678 Sq. Ft. – Second Floor
17,712 Cu. Ft.

Perhaps more than any other design in recent years the A-frame has captured the imagination of the prospective vacation home builder. There is a gala air about its shape that fosters a holiday spirit whether the house be a summer retreat or a structure for year 'round living. This particular A-frame offers a lot of living, for there are five bedrooms, two baths, an efficient kitchen, a family-dining area, and outstanding storage. As in most designs of this type, the living room, with its great height and large glass area, is extremely dramatic.

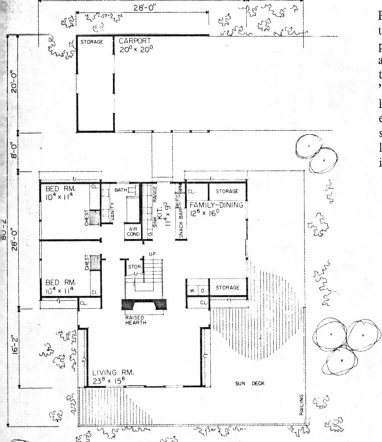

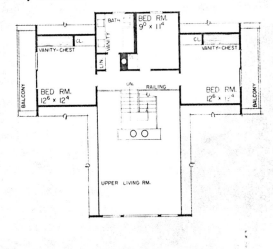

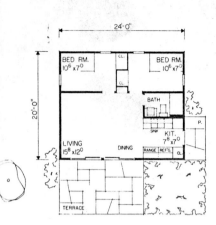

Design S 1486
480 Sq. Ft./4,118 Cu. Ft.

You'll be anxious to start building this delightful little vacation home. Whether you do-it-yourself, or engage professional help, you'll not have to wait long for its completion.

Design S 2425
1,106 Sq. Ft. / 14,599 Cu. Ft.

You'll adjust to living in this vacation cottage with the greatest of ease. And for evermore the byword will be, "fun". Imagine, a thirty-one foot living room!

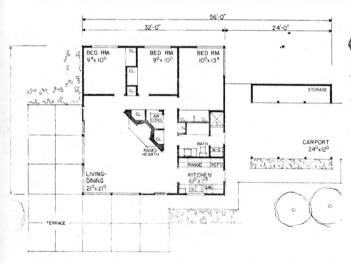

Design S 1449
1,024 Sq. Ft./11,264 Cu. Ft.

If yours is a preference for a vacation home with a distinctive flair, then you need not look any further. Here is a simple and economically built 32 foot rectangle.

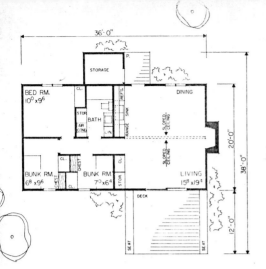

Design S 1488
720 Sq. Ft./8,518 Cu. Ft.

The kids won't be able to move into this vacation retreat soon enough. And neither will the housewife whose housekeeping will be almost non-existent. A real leisure-time home.

Design S 1462
1,176 Sq. Ft. / 11,995 Cu. Ft.

A second home with the informal living message readily apparent both inside and out. The zoning of this home is indeed most interesting — and practical, too. Study the plan carefully.

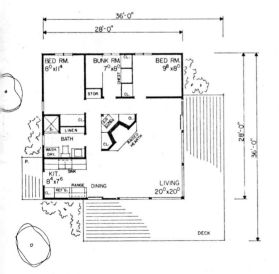

Here's a perfect 28 foot square that will surely open up new dimensions in living for its occupants. A fine, lower budget version of S 1449 on opposing page.

Design S 1485
784 Sq. Ft./10,192 Cu. Ft.

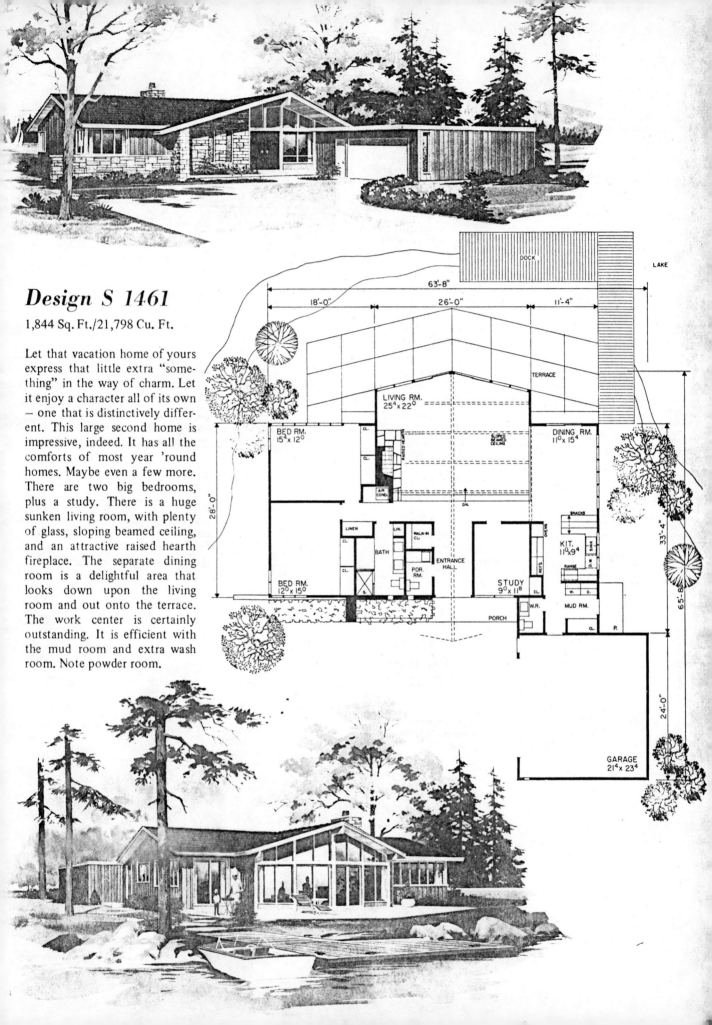

Design S 1461

1,844 Sq. Ft./21,798 Cu. Ft.

Let that vacation home of yours express that little extra "something" in the way of charm. Let it enjoy a character all of its own — one that is distinctively different. This large second home is impressive, indeed. It has all the comforts of most year 'round homes. Maybe even a few more. There are two big bedrooms, plus a study. There is a huge sunken living room, with plenty of glass, sloping beamed ceiling, and an attractive raised hearth fireplace. The separate dining room is a delightful area that looks down upon the living room and out onto the terrace. The work center is certainly outstanding. It is efficient with the mud room and extra wash room. Note powder room.

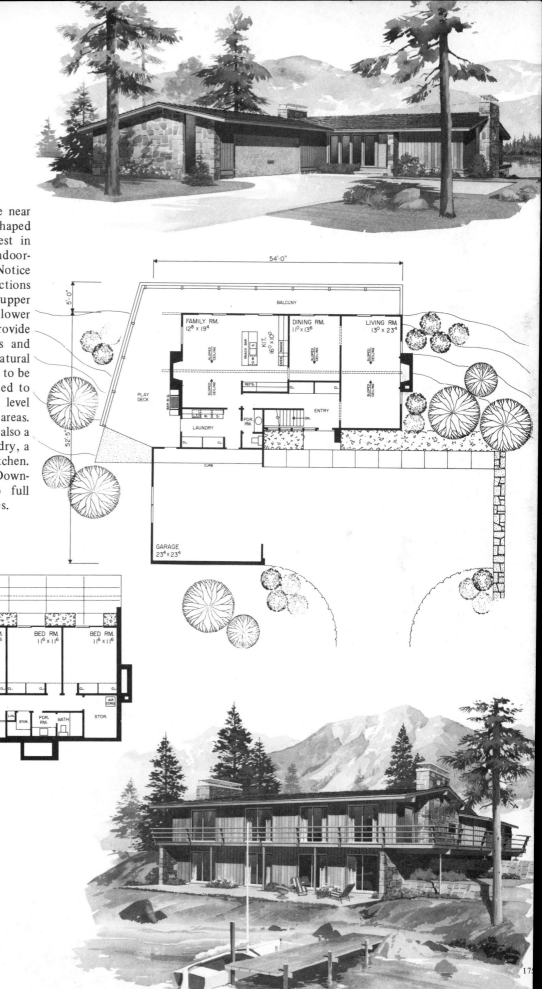

Design S 2205

1,229 Sq. Ft. – Upper Level
1,229 Sq. Ft. – Lower Level
23,351 Cu. Ft.

Whether your sloping site be near the lakeshore or not, this L-shaped hillside design offers the best in gracious living. What fine indoor-outdoor relationships it has! Notice how every major room functions with either the deck of the upper level or the terrace of the lower level. Sliding glass doors provide easy access to the outdoors and permits an abundance of natural light inside. If there is a view to be enjoyed, it may be appreciated to the very fullest. The upper level highlights two spacious living areas. Each has a fireplace. There is also a separate dining room, a laundry, a powder room and an open kitchen. Notice the sloping ceilings. Downstairs, four bedrooms, two full baths, and fine storage facilities.

Design S 2430

1,238 Sq. Ft. – First Floor
648 Sq. Ft. – Second Floor
18,743 Cu. Ft.

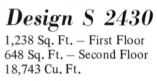

Design S 2427

784 Sq. Ft. — First Floor
504 Sq. Ft. — Second Floor
13,485 Cu. Ft.

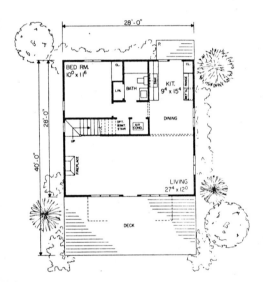 

If ever a design had "vacation home" written all over it, this one has! Perhaps the most carefree characteristic of all is the second floor balcony which looks down upon the wood deck. This balcony provides the outdoor living facility for the big master bedroom. Also occupying the second floor is the kids' dormitory. The use of bunks would be a fine utilization of this space. Panels through the knee walls give access to abundant storage area. Downstairs there is yet another bedroom, a bath, a 27 foot living room.

Design S 1482

1,008 Sq. Ft. — First Floor
637 Sq. Ft. — Second Floor
16,657 Cu. Ft.

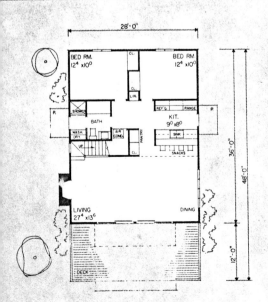 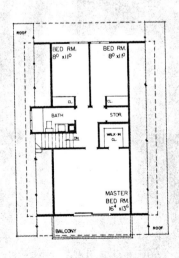

Here's a chalet right from the pages of the travel folders. Whether the setting reflects the majestic beauty of a winter scene, or the tranquil splendor of a summer landscape, this design will serve its occupants well. In addition to the big bedrooms on the first floor, there are three more upstairs. The large master bedroom has a balcony which looks down upon the lower wood deck. There are two full baths. The first floor bath is directly accessible from the outdoors. The kitchen is but a step from the side yard. Note snack bar, pantry, laundry area.

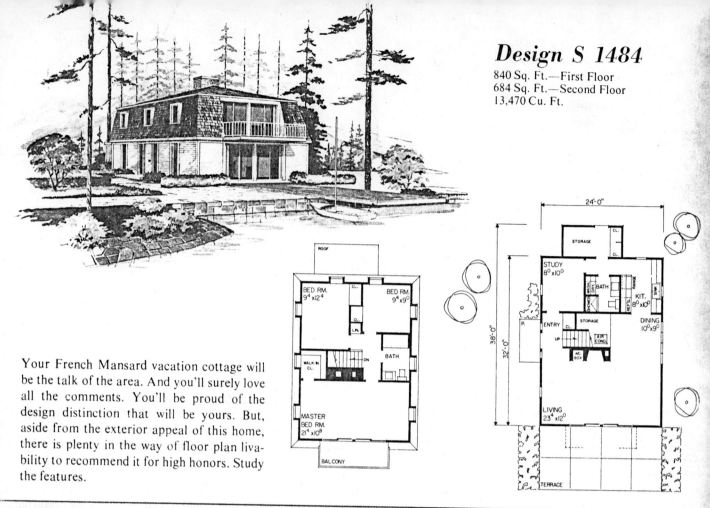

Design S 1484

840 Sq. Ft.—First Floor
684 Sq. Ft.—Second Floor
13,470 Cu. Ft.

ROOF

BED RM.
9⁴ x12⁴

CL.

BED RM.
9⁴ x9⁰

CL.

L.PN.

WALK IN
CL.

DN

BATH

MASTER
BED RM.
21⁴ x10⁸

BALCONY

24'-0"

STORAGE

CL.

CL.

STUDY
8⁰ x10⁰

WASH. DRY.

BATH

RANGE

KIT.
8⁰ x10⁰

REF.

SINK

ENTRY

UP

STORAGE

DINING
10⁰ x9⁰

CL.

AIR COND.

WD. BOX

P.

38'-0"

32'-0"

LIVING
23⁴ x12⁰

TERRACE

Your French Mansard vacation cottage will be the talk of the area. And you'll surely love all the comments. You'll be proud of the design distinction that will be yours. But, aside from the exterior appeal of this home, there is plenty in the way of floor plan livability to recommend it for high honors. Study the features.

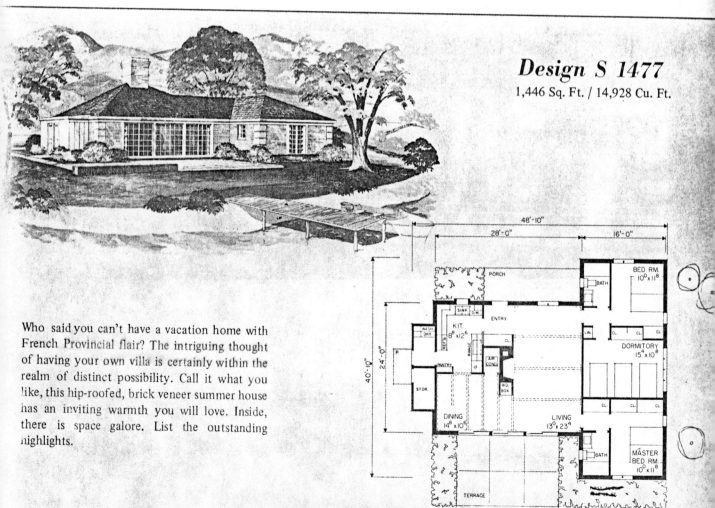

Design S 1477

1,446 Sq. Ft. / 14,928 Cu. Ft.

48'-10"

28'-0"

16'-0"

PORCH

BED RM.
10⁰ x11⁸

BATH

SINK
D.W.

ENTRY

WASH. DRY.

REF.

KIT.
8⁶ x12⁶

RANGE

CL.

L.PN.

CL.

CL.

CL.

DORMITORY
15⁴ x10⁸

P.

PANTRY

AIR COND.

WD. BOX

STOR.

40'-10"

24'-0"

DINING
14⁸ x10⁵

LIVING
13⁰ x23⁴

CL.

CL.

CL.

CL.

BATH

MASTER
BED RM.
10⁰ x11⁸

TERRACE

Who said you can't have a vacation home with French Provincial flair? The intriguing thought of having your own villa is certainly within the realm of distinct possibility. Call it what you like, this hip-roofed, brick veneer summer house has an inviting warmth you will love. Inside, there is space galore. List the outstanding highlights.

Design S 1483

816 Sq. Ft. — First Floor
642 Sq. Ft. — Second Floor
13,513 Cu. Ft.

Take the charm of early America to the lake-shore with you. The graciousness of this little gambrel-roofed vacation home will be with you always. In fact, it will improve with age. The narrow, horizontal siding, the wide corner boards, the projecting dormers, the muntined windows, and the center chimney create an aura of authenticity. Observe the outstanding livability.

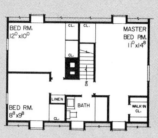

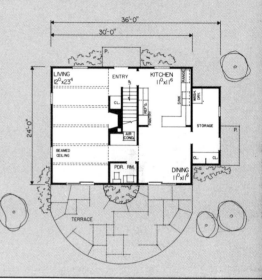

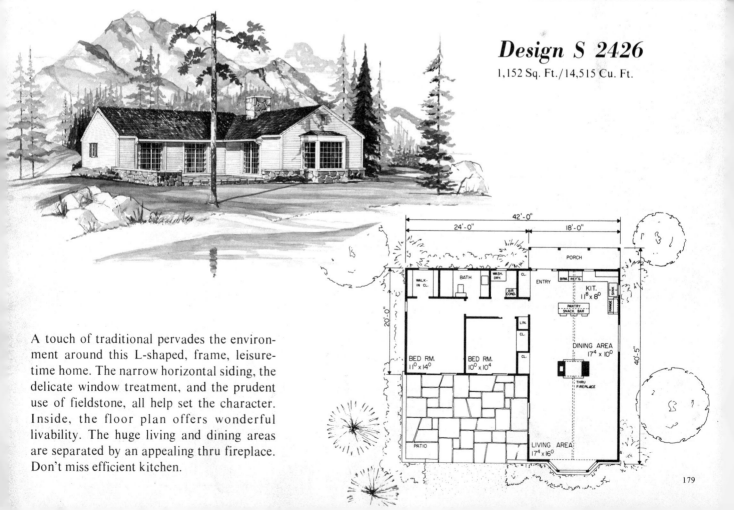

Design S 2426

1,152 Sq. Ft./14,515 Cu. Ft.

A touch of traditional pervades the environment around this L-shaped, frame, leisure-time home. The narrow horizontal siding, the delicate window treatment, and the prudent use of fieldstone, all help set the character. Inside, the floor plan offers wonderful livability. The huge living and dining areas are separated by an appealing thru fireplace. Don't miss efficient kitchen.

179

Design S 2459

1,264 Sq. Ft. — First Floor
556 Sq. Ft. — Second Floor
18,587 Cu. Ft.

Dramatic, indeed! The soaring roof projects and heightens the appeal of the slanted glass gable end. The expanse of the roof is broken to provide access to the side deck from the dining room. Above is the balcony of the second floor lounge. This room with its high sloping ceiling looks down on the first floor living room. The master bedroom also has an outdoor balcony. Back downstairs there are loads of features. They include two large bedrooms, a big dining room and a huge living room.

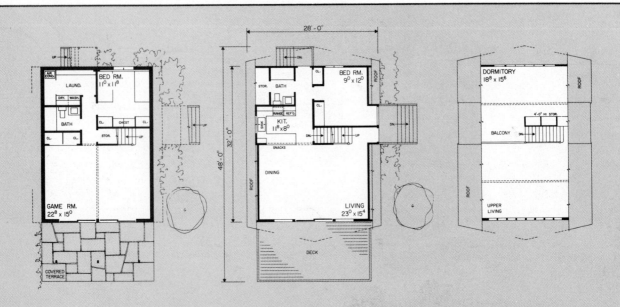

Design S 2431

1,057 Sq. Ft. – First Floor
406 Sq. Ft. – Second Floor/26,529 Cu. Ft.

A favorite everywhere – the A-frame vacation home. Its popularity is easily discernible. The stately appearance is enhanced by the soaring roof lines and the dramatic glass areas. Inside, the breathtaking beauty of outstanding architectural detailing is also apparent. The high ceiling of the living room slopes and has exposed beams. The second floor master suite is a great feature. Observe the raised hearth fireplace and the outdoor balcony. This outdoor spot will certainly be a quiet perch for sun bathing.

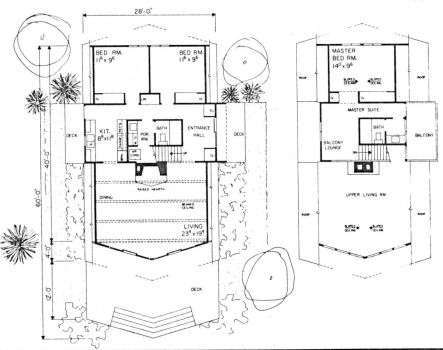

Design S 1499

896 Sq. Ft. – Main Level/298 Sq. Ft. – Upper Level
896 Sq. Ft. – Lower Level/18,784 Cu. Ft.

Three level living results in family living patterns which will foster a delightful feeling of informality. Upon his arrival at this charming second home, each family member will enthusiastically welcome the change in environment – both indoors and out. Whether looking down into the living room from the dormitory balcony, or walking through the sliding doors onto the huge deck, or participating in some family activity in the game room, everyone will count the hours spent here as relaxing ones. Study the plan carefully.

Design S 1453

1,476 Sq. Ft./13,934 Cu. Ft.

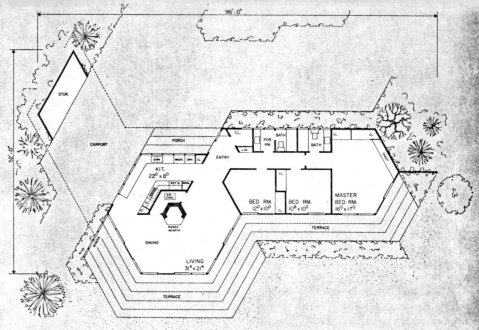

An exciting design, unusual in character, yet fun to live in. This frame home, with its vertical siding and large glass areas, has as its dramatic focal point a hexagonal living area which gives way to interesting angles. The large living area features sliding glass doors through which traffic may pass to the terrace stretching across the entire length of the house. The wide overhanging roof projects over the terrace and results in a large covered area outside the sliding doors of the master bedroom.

Design S 1404   1,336 Sq. Ft./12,230 Cu. Ft.

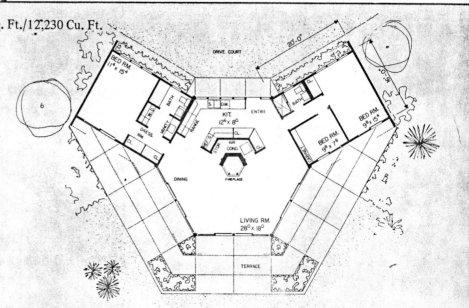

Designed for pleasingly different and carefree living patterns. The main living area is a hexagon featuring delightful open planning. Living and dining will revolve around the attractive and strategically located fireplace above which the sloping ceilings converge. Two projecting wings provide the sleeping facilities. Each has a full bath — one with tub, the other with stall shower. The kitchen is well-planned and efficient in which to function. Sliding glass doors provide access from the bedrooms and living area to the huge terrace. Observe the wide overhanging, protective roof.

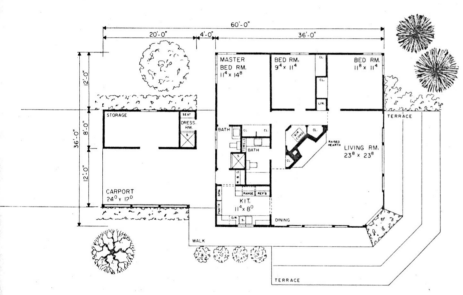

Design S 2457

1,288 Sq. Ft./13,730 Cu. Ft.

Leisure living will indeed be graciously experienced in this hip-roofed second home. Except for the clipped corner, it is a perfect square measuring 36 x 36 feet. The 23 foot square living room enjoys a great view of the surrounding environment by virtue of the expanses of glass. The wide overhanging roof affords protection from the sun. The "open planning" adds to the spaciousness of the interior. The focal point is the raised hearth fireplace. The three bedrooms are served by two full baths also accessible to other areas.

Design S 2412

1,120 Sq. Ft. — First Floor
664 Sq. Ft. — Second Floor
18,680 Cu. Ft.

It will make no difference where you locate this chalet-type second home. The atmosphere it creates will be one for true leisure living. To guarantee sheer enjoyment you wouldn't even have to be situated close to the water. And little wonder with such an array of features as: the big deck, the fine porch, and the two balconies. For complete livability there are four bedrooms, two full baths, an outstanding U-shaped kitchen, a large living area with a raised fireplace, and a super-abundance of closet and storage facilities. Of particular interest is the direct access from outdoors to the first floor bath with its stall shower.

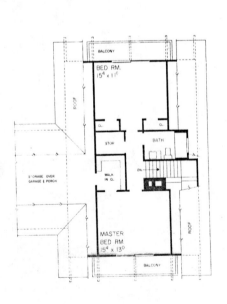

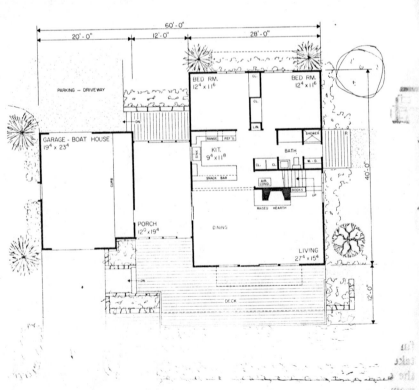

Design S 1475

1,120 Sq. Ft. – First Floor/522 Sq. Ft. – Second Floor/616 Sq. Ft. – Lounge Level/24,406 Cu. Ft.

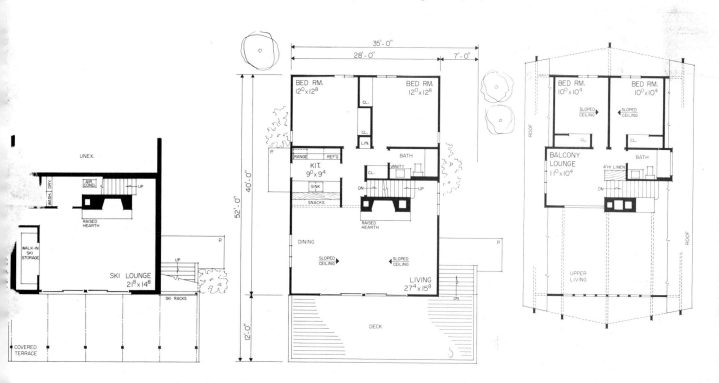

Skiers take notice! This vacation home tells an exciting story of activity — and people. Whether you build this design to function as your ski lodge, or to serve your family and friends during the summer months, it will perform ideally. It would [take] little imagination to envision this second home overlooking your lakeshore site with the grownups sunning themselves on [the] deck while the children play on the terrace. Whatever the season, or the location, visualize how your family will enjoy the [many] hours spent in this delightful chalet adaptation.

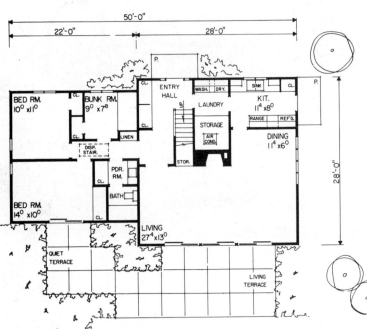

Design S 1481

1,268 Sq. Ft.—First Floor
700 Sq. Ft.—Second Floor
18,112 Cu. Ft.

Here are three second homes that retain much of the form, or shape, of traditional New England design to which has been added present day window treatment. The result is a pleasing mixture of the old and the new. Study the plans carefully. Livability is exceptional.

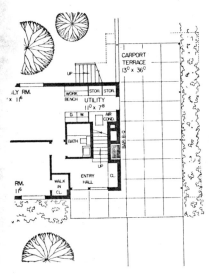

Design S 1445

)60 Sq. Ft. – Upper Level/628 Sq. Ft. – Lower Level/15,304 Cu. Ft.

Vhy not give two-level living a try and make your leisure-time home something delightfully different. If there is plenty of countryside or water around, you'll love viewing it from the upper level. And the best seat in the house will not be inside at all, but out on the balcony or deck.

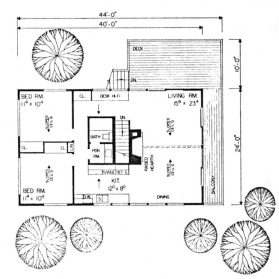

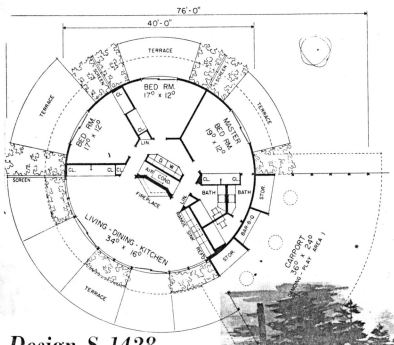

Design S 1428

1,256 Sq. Ft./12,975 Cu. Ft.

A round house is ideal for a light-hearted atmosphere, and what better spot for the light-in-heart than a vacation home? Terraces surround its circumference, accessible from each portion of the living and sleeping areas through sliding glass doors. The living area, with its strip kitchen and dining space, flares out from the dramatic fireplace with its raised hearth.

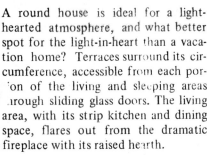

Design S 1478

1,156 Sq. Ft.—First Floor
596 Sq. Ft.—Second Floor
15,656 Cu. Ft.

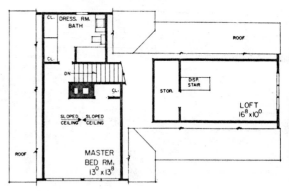

Here is an abundance of vacation livability. Well zoned, there is a spacious beamed ceiling and dining area, an exceptional work center, a separate first floor sleeping wing. Upstairs there is the elegant master bedroom suite. For extra space don't miss the loft.

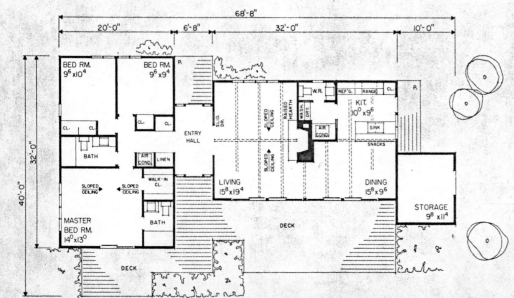

Design S 1479

1,360 Sq. Ft./17,026 Cu. Ft.

This unique plan is basically two 20 x 32 foot rectangles connected by an entrance hall, or passage unit. A sweeping wood deck provides the common outdoor living area. The sleeping unit has three bedrooms and two full baths. The ceiling of the master bedroom slopes.

..ABOUT YOUR HOME PLANNERS BLUEPRINTS

The development of each house from the preliminary design and planning stages through the complete architectural drawings and artist's landscaped rendering is always an exciting experience for the creative staff of Home Planners. Many capable people and many man-hours are required to complete this interesting professional work.

Home Planners takes pride in providing complete blueprint packages that include all the "tools" you and your builder need for the selection and specification of your materials and equipment, for estimating the costs and the actual construction of your new home.

THE CONSTRUCTION PLANS

Our attractive and sturdy mailing carton with blueprints, material lists and specification outline enclosed provides a handy storage file for your complete blueprint package and other miscellaneous items you may accumulate in planning your new home. A typical set of blueprints is illustrated on the next page. Because of the size, the style, and the type of home for which you may order blueprints, the number of sheets comprising your set of blueprints may vary. The blueprint sets for the designs in this book contain from five to ten sheets.

THE MATERIALS LIST

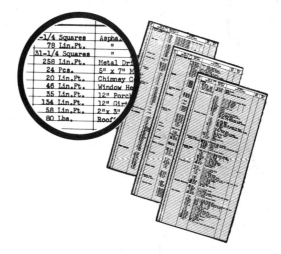

THE SPECIFICATION OUTLINE

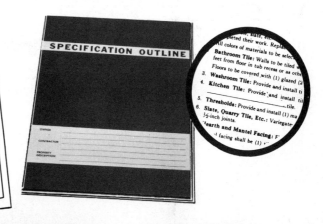

DESIGN #1446 © HOME PLANNERS, INC., DETROIT

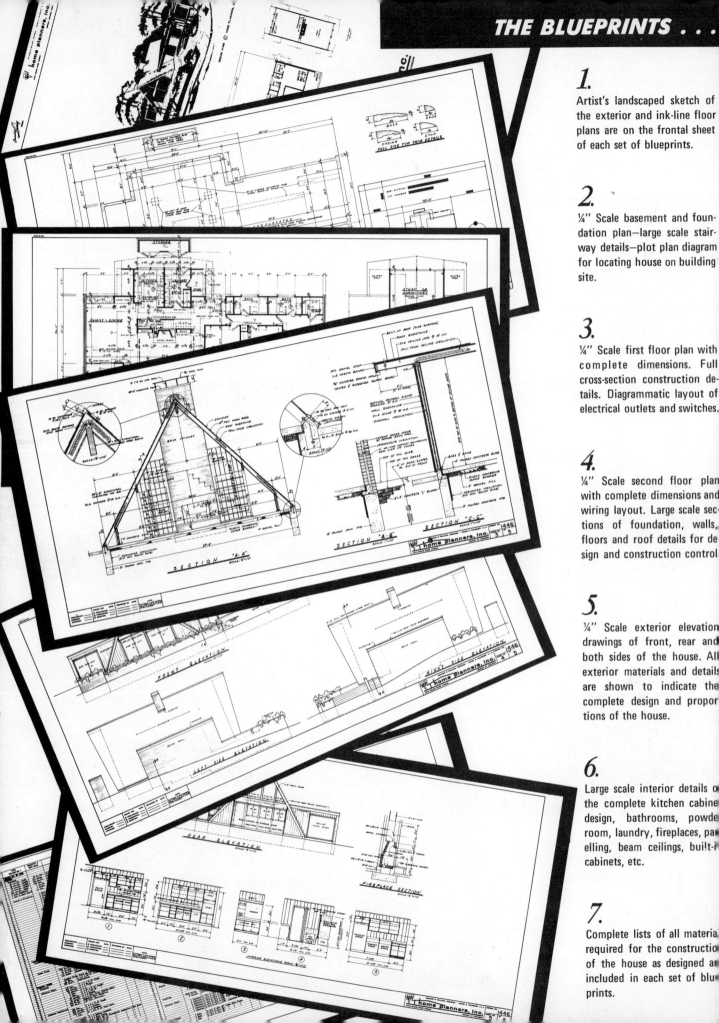

1.

Artist's landscaped sketch of the exterior and ink-line floor plans are on the frontal sheet of each set of blueprints.

2.

¼" Scale basement and foundation plan—large scale stairway details—plot plan diagram for locating house on building site.

3.

¼" Scale first floor plan with complete dimensions. Full cross-section construction details. Diagrammatic layout of electrical outlets and switches.

4.

¼" Scale second floor plan with complete dimensions and wiring layout. Large scale sections of foundation, walls, floors and roof details for design and construction control

5.

¼" Scale exterior elevation drawings of front, rear and both sides of the house. All exterior materials and details are shown to indicate the complete design and proportions of the house.

6.

Large scale interior details of the complete kitchen cabinet design, bathrooms, powder room, laundry, fireplaces, panelling, beam ceilings, built-in cabinets, etc.

7.

Complete lists of all material required for the construction of the house as designed are included in each set of blueprints.

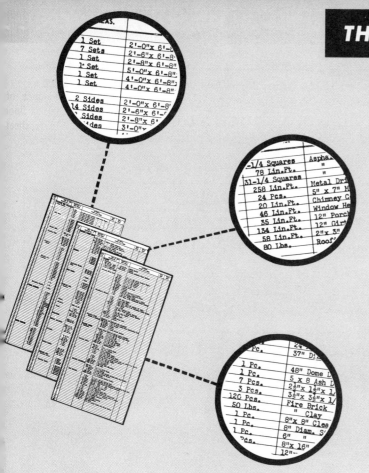

THE MATERIAL LIST...

With each set of blueprints you order you will receive a material list. Each list shows you the quantity, type and size of the non-mechanical materials required to build your home. It also tells you where these materials are used. This makes the blueprints easy to understand.

Influencing the mechanical requirements are geographical differences in availability of materials, local codes, methods of installation and individual preferences. Because of these factors, your local heating, plumbing and electrical contractors can supply you with necessary material take-offs for their particular trades.

Material lists simplify your material ordering and enable you to get quicker price quotations from your builder and material dealer. Because the material list is an integral part of each set of blueprints, they are not available separately.

Among the materials listed:
- **Masonry, Veneer & Fireplace • Framing Lumber • Roofing & Sheet Metal • Windows & Door Frames • Exterior Trim & Insulation • Tile Work, Finish Floors • Interior Trim, Kitchen Cabinets • Rough & Finish Hardware**

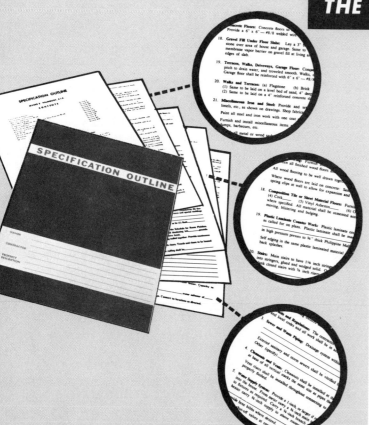

THE SPECIFICATION OUTLINE...

This fill-in type specification lists over 150 phases of home construction from excavating to painting and includes wiring, plumbing, heating and air-conditioning. It consists of 16 pages and will prove invaluable for specifying to your builder the exact materials, equipment and methods of construction you want in your new home.

One Specification Outline is included free with each order for blueprints. Additional Specification Outlines are available at $2.00 each.

CONTENTS

- **General Instructions, Suggestions and Information • Excavating and Grading • Masonry and Concrete Work • Sheet Metal Work • Carpentry, Millwork, Roofing, and Miscellaneous Items • Lath and Plaster or Drywall Wallboard • Schedule for Room Finishes • Painting and Finishing • Tile Work • Electrical Work • Plumbing • Heating and Air Conditioning**

For Your Ordering Convenience –

**CLIP THIS COUPON
AND MAIL TODAY!**

→

*In Canada Mail To:
Home Planners, Inc.
772 King St. W.
Kitchener, Ontario
N2G 1E8*

TO: Home Planners, Inc. • **16310 Grand River Ave.** • **Detroit, Michigan 48227**

Please rush me the following

_____ BLUEPRINTS FOR DESIGNS   #_____   #_____   #_____   #_____ $_____

Single Set $40.00, Additional Identical Sets in Same Order $10.00 ea.
(Material Lists and 1 Specification Outline included)

_____ SPECIFICATION OUTLINES @ $2.00 EACH .... $_____

Michigan Residents add 4% sales tax $_____

$_____

FOR POSTAGE
AND HANDLING
PLEASE CHECK
✔ & REMIT

☐ $1.00 Added to Order for Surface Mail — Any Mdse.
☐ $1.50 Added for Air Mail of One Set of Blueprints only.
☐ $3.00 Added for Air Mail of Two or more Sets of Blueprints only.
☐ For Foreign Mail add $1.00 to above applicable rates.

☐ C.O.D. PAY POSTMAN (C.O.D. Within U.S.A. Only)   TOTAL in U.S.A. funds .... $_____

Name_____

Address_____

City_____ State_____ Zip_____

BSHP

Prices subject to change without notice

ALL BLUEPRINT ORDERS SHIPPED WITHIN 48-HOURS!

**CLIP THIS COUPON
AND MAIL TODAY!**

→

*In Canada Mail To:
Home Planners, Inc.
772 King St. W.
Kitchener, Ontario
N2G 1E8*

TO: Home Planners, Inc. • **16310 Grand River Ave.** • **Detroit, Michigan 48227**

Please rush me the following

_____ BLUEPRINTS FOR DESIGNS   #_____   #_____   #_____   #_____ $_____

Single Set $40.00, Additional Identical Sets in Same Order $10.00 ea.
(Material Lists and 1 Specification Outline included)

_____ SPECIFICATION OUTLINES @ $2.00 EACH .... $_____

Michigan Residents add 4% sales tax $_____

$_____

FOR POSTAGE
AND HANDLING
PLEASE CHECK
✔ & REMIT

☐ $1.00 Added to Order for Surface Mail — Any Mdse.
☐ $1.50 Added for Air Mail of One Set of Blueprints only.
☐ $3.00 Added for Air Mail of Two or more Sets of Blueprints only.
☐ For Foreign Mail add $1.00 to above applicable rates.

☐ C.O.D. PAY POSTMAN (C.O.D. Within U.S.A. Only)   TOTAL in U.S.A. funds .... $_____

Name_____

Address_____

City_____ State_____ Zip_____

BSHP

Prices subject to change without notice

ALL BLUEPRINT ORDERS SHIPPED WITHIN 48-HOURS!

**CLIP THIS COUPON
AND MAIL TODAY!**

→

*In Canada Mail To:
Home Planners, Inc.
772 King St. W.
Kitchener, Ontario
N2G 1E8*

TO: Home Planners, Inc. • **16310 Grand River Ave.** • **Detroit, Michigan 48227**

Please rush me the following

_____ BLUEPRINTS FOR DESIGNS   #_____   #_____   #_____   #_____ $_____

Single Set $40.00, Additional Identical Sets in Same Order $10.00 ea.
(Material Lists and 1 Specification Outline included)

_____ SPECIFICATION OUTLINES @ $2.00 EACH .... $_____

Michigan Residents add 4% sales tax $_____

$_____

FOR POSTAGE
AND HANDLING
PLEASE CHECK
✔ & REMIT

☐ $1.00 Added to Order for Surface Mail — Any Mdse.
☐ $1.50 Added for Air Mail of One Set of Blueprints only.
☐ $3.00 Added for Air Mail of Two or more Sets of Blueprints only.
☐ For Foreign Mail add $1.00 to above applicable rates.

☐ C.O.D. PAY POSTMAN (C.O.D. Within U.S.A. Only)   TOTAL in U.S.A. funds .... $_____

Name_____

Address_____

City_____ State_____ Zip_____

BSHP

Prices subject to change without notice

ALL BLUEPRINT ORDERS SHIPPED WITHIN 48-HOURS!